50

Shades of

Power

Manhardeep Singh

Contents

Introduction

"Do not pray for an easy life, pray for the strength to endure one."

Bruce Lee

In a world ruled by power and control, where some people hold the reins and others try to break free, one question has been on people's minds since the beginning of time: What does it really mean to possess power? As we start this journey to understand what power is and how it works, I can't help but think of what Bruce Lee said. Power isn't just something that's given to us; it's a force that comes from going through hard times and not giving up. Power has shaped empires, changed the paths of people's lives, and changed the course of history. And as we look deeper into the world of power and control, we'll start to see how complicated and nuanced it is.

From ancient stories about kings and conquerors to modern battles for power in boardrooms and on battlefields, our world is full of stories about power and its effects. Yet, in a world where power dynamics are everywhere, we often find ourselves confused and overwhelmed by how complicated they are. How do some people easily get the attention and respect of others, while others are stuck in a position where they have no power? How can we find our way through the maze-like corridors of power without getting lost? These questions make us want to know more and push us to look for answers that go beyond what we already know.

Many people who want to learn about power look for simple explanations and oversimplified theories, which often give them a skewed view of what power is really about. They use worn out ideas about power, like associating it only with dominance or force, and they don't understand the subtleties and nuances that build its expressions. Others fall for the appeal of quick fixes, hoping to get power by taking short cuts or manipulating others, only to get caught in a web of lies and disappointment. The pursuit of power is not a game that should be taken lightly. It requires a deep understanding of all of its complexities and a firm commitment to using it in a responsible way.

In the pages that follow, I want to take you on an enlightening journey as we look at the 50 Shades of Power in our world. This is not a book about tricks or short cuts to power. Instead, it is a nuanced and thorough look at all the different kinds of power. We'll use psychology, history, sociology, and philosophy, along with other fields, to figure out how power works and reveal the hidden mechanisms that make it happen.

Power will no longer be a hard-to-grasp idea shrouded in mystery and apprehension. Through insightful analysis, interesting stories, and useful advice, we will take the mystery out of power and give you the tools you need to navigate the complicated world of authority and influence. This isn't a book for people who are ruthless or conniving. Instead, it's a compass for people who want to understand how power works so they can make real changes in their personal and professional lives.

I know that you really want to understand how power works. It's not just an intellectual pursuit; it's about finding out more about yourself. We are naturally drawn to power because it shapes our relationships and determines our futures. But power is a double-edged sword that can do both great good and terrible things. So, it is important that we start this journey together, hand in hand, so that we can navigate the complicated terrain of power with integrity and purpose.

Imagine a world where power didn't lead to corruption and oppression, but instead sparked good things to happen. Imagine a world where people with power use it with grace and wisdom, making others want to be great and lighting the fire of their true potential. This is the kind of world we will try to build with the knowledge and insights we gain on this journey of transformation.

In the pages that follow, I promise to take you on a thrilling journey through history, telling you about powerful leaders, master manipulators, and unexpected heroes who used different kinds of power to change the course of humanity. Together, we'll figure out what power play is all about, including all of its subtleties and hidden strategies. Get ready, because you're about to go on an exciting adventure. Once you've read 50 Shades of Power the world will never look the same again.

Chapter One

The Foundation of Power

The Nature of Power

Power. It is a word that echoes with authority, ambition, and influence. It is an abstract concept, but it affects every part of our lives in a real way. Power shows up in many different ways, from the pursuit of personal goals to the shaping of societies. It is a complex thread that runs through all of human life. But, what exactly is power?

At its core, power is the ability to control and affect other people. It is what drives people to reach their goals, navigate their relationships, and shape their outcomes. It is the subtle dance of manipulation, the enticing allure of dominance, and the thing that makes change happen. It is a force that can be both good and bad, depending on what its user wants to do and how they use it.

We can't say enough about how important power is in our lives. It's what keeps us going and keeps us moving forward on the journey of life. Power is the thing that helps us get past problems, overcome challenges, and get what we really want. It is the key to inspiring others and getting them to work together towards a common goal. Power is the currency of influence. It gives us the chance to shape the world around us and leave our mark on history.

But power is not one entity; it is more like a gem with many different sides that reflect the light from many different sources. People can use their wealth, knowledge, social status, and physical strength, among other things, to get what they want. Each source of power has its own strengths and weaknesses, as well as its own way of changing people's hearts and minds.

But power is not just a force from the outside. It starts with us, with our ability to make and control our own choices and actions. I've learned that personal power is the foundation on which every other type of power is built. It shows that a person is self-aware and has self-discipline. It shows that a person knows that true power doesn't come from being able to control others, but from being able to control themselves.

On the other hand, positional power comes from a person's role or position in a hierarchy. It is a power that is given to someone instead of earned, and it has its own set of pros and cons. Expert power, on the other hand, comes from being an expert and knowing a lot about a certain subject. It is a power that comes from knowing how to do something well, and it is typically accompanied with respect and admiration.

But respect and admiration are not the only ways to get power. There are also ways to have power based on fear and coercion. For example, coercive power uses force, threats, or punishments to keep people in line. It's a power that can quickly destroy trust and make people resentful, so it's important to think carefully about its moral implications. In the same way, reward power is the ability to give people incentives to change their minds. But relying on reward power can have its own problems. It can lead to a transactional and superficial way of dealing with people.

Referent power, on the other hand, comes from a person's charisma, charm, and ability to get along with other people. It is a power that can be grown and nourished by making real connections and being emotionally intelligent. Another kind of power is network power, which depends on a person's ability to access and use social networks and connections. It is a power that comes from being able to make connections and form alliances, which gives you opportunities to have influence and control.

Moral power, on the other hand, comes from a person's moral principles and values. It's a power that comes from doing things that are in line with your morals and make other people want to do the same. Situational power comes from certain circumstances or situations, as the name suggests. It is a power that can come and go, so you have to be aware of the environment and be able to adapt quickly.

On the other hand, informal power comes from personal connections, networks, and alliances. It is a power that isn't often seen or talked about, but it can have a lot of control and influence. The norms, values, and beliefs of a society give rise to cultural power. It shapes and affects people and groups, and often sets the limits and possibilities of power in a society.

But the real key to having influence and control is how these different kinds of power work together. By putting together different shades of power, you can create a symphony of influence that helps navigate complicated situations and reach goals. It's a delicate dance that requires knowing a lot about yourself and the way power works.

Power, on the other hand, is not a simple force; it is a complex and dynamic phenomenon. It goes up and down and changes to fit new situations and relationships. To find your way through the complicated world of power, you need to keep learning, be flexible, and always be committed to using it responsibly.

The Psychology of Power

In the depths of my research into the world of power, I have looked into the complex psychological web that makes it work. It's both interesting and scary because it peels back the layers of the human mind and shows the basic instincts that make us want power.

I can't say enough about how important it is to understand the psychology of power dynamics, because that's how we can start to understand how much it affects our lives. Whether we know it or not, power affects our relationships, the choices we make, and even our sense of who we are.

The basic human instinct for dominance lies at the heart of the psychology of power. From ancient tribal societies to the modern world, people have always had a strong desire for power. It's a result of evolution, based on the instinct to survive that drove our ancestors to set up hierarchies and show who was in charge.

But what drives this instinct for power? What drives us to seek control and influence over our fellow beings? The answers lie in the human mind, which is a complicated mix of desires, fears, and emotions.

Perception, especially of power, is a big part of how power struggles play out and what happens as a result. How both those with power and those who are ruled by it see it can have a big effect on how things go in terms of power. It can make a difference in how people use power and whether it leads to cooperation or conflict.

To really understand how power works, we need to look to the field of social psychology. This field looks at the theories and experiments that explain how power works and shows how complicated it can be. It shows the power of social influence and how power shapes our thoughts, actions, and feelings.

Power has a big effect on people because it can change who they are at their core. Power can give you a sense of confidence and control, but it can also make you arrogant and distant. On the other hand, being under someone in charge can make you feel weak and submissive, or it can make you want to rebel and break free.

The strange psychology of power and control is part of the realm of power. What motivates people to seek dominance? What are the psychological processes that make people want to be influential? The answers lie in the complicated way that dominance, authority, and the winding paths of the human mind all work together.

Power is not a separate force; it is a part of who we are. Power dynamics may adjust and be changed by things like gender, race, and social status. The way power is shared in society is a reflection of the beliefs and biases that make up our society as a whole. It is always there and shapes our experiences, our opportunities, and even our sense of who we are.

So, people in power use psychology as a way to keep and strengthen their power. Some of the ways that power is kept are through manipulation, persuasion, and psychological warfare. The study of psychology shows how people in power use strategies to make sure they don't lose control.

But there is also resistance to power. There are psychological reasons why people defy authority, rebel, and try to change the way things are. Defiance and rebellion are the ways that power structures are broken and that people who don't have a voice are given one.

But power doesn't just come from the people who use it. It also lives in people who voluntarily give in to it. The psychology of followership explains why and how people submit to power, whether out of duty, loyalty, or a desire for security.

Unfortunately, power can also be a force of evil. In abusive relationships, power is used to control, manipulate, and make the other person afraid. The psychology of abusive power dynamics reveals the dark undercurrents of these kinds of relationships and shows how manipulation and control keep abusive power structures in place.

Power dynamics can happen in organizations as well. Leadership, hierarchy, and the psychology of the workplace all affect the way power works in an organization. In these kinds of organizational settings, the psychology of power can lead to cooperation, conflict, or a toxic environment of dominance and suppression.

Power can and does play a role in decision-making. The psychology of power can make it hard to make good decisions, which can lead to cognitive biases, groupthink, and the abuse of power. To make ethical decisions and stop power abuse, it's important to understand these psychological factors.

But power can also be a force for change in society. Activism, social movements, and the search for social justice are all fueled by the way power works. The psychology behind these movements shows the passion, conviction, and sheer will that drive people to challenge the power structures that are already in place.

You can't ignore what powerlessness does to your mind. Having power and control over you can have big effects on your mind. Learned helplessness, psychological trauma, and feeling like a victim are just a few of the things that can happen to people who feel like they have no control.

Power dynamics are also linked to empathy. How power affects our ability to understand what other people are going through is a key part of our relationships, our ability to understand, and our ability to create a fair and caring world.

Power and morality walk together on a treacherous path. The moral implications of power dynamics have a long-lasting effect on the decisions and actions we make. Power has the potential to make people do undesirable things and compromise their morals. To keep ethics from falling apart, it's important to understand these psychological factors.

Power affects every part of our minds because it can change the way we see ourselves. Power can boost self-esteem and self-efficacy, but it can also undermine our sense of self-worth. The psychology of power and self-perception is connected to how we see ourselves, what we believe, and what we want to achieve.

When it comes to relationships between people, power dynamics are the most important thing. Whether it's a romantic relationship, a friendship, or a family bond, the rise and fall of power affects all of them. To make healthy connections and keep things in balance, it's important to understand the psychological dynamics of these relationships.

Power dynamics affect how we interact with each other, how we act, and how much we feel like we belong in a group. The invisible threads of power have an effect on social influence, conformity, and how people act in groups. The psychology of power and group dynamics reveals the hidden currents that run through our lives as a group.

These are merely a few of the numerous shades of power that color our world. Power is a complex, many-sided thing that is woven into the fabric of our lives. It is a force that goes up and down, changes, and flows with the tides of life and the landscapes of the mind.

The Laws of Power

Power is a force that controls our lives and shapes how we act, who we are, and where we stand in society. It is like an invisible thread that runs through every part of our lives and has an effect on both people and institutions. In my previous exploration of power dynamics, I delved into the psychological underpinnings of power and control. Now we'll talk about the Laws of Power, which are the universal rules that govern how people get and use power. Anyone who wants to get along well in the complicated world of power needs to know these laws.

At its core, the Laws of Power are a set of rules that explain how power works and how people use it. They give you a way to think about what it takes to get power, use power, and keep power. These laws are universal because they are based on timeless truths about human nature and the way people interact with each other. If you don't follow the Laws of Power, you'll be blindly navigating the dangerous waters of power and subject to its whims. But if you accept these laws, you give yourself the knowledge and tools you need to shape your own future.

The Law of Influence:

The Law of Influence is the first law of power. Influence is the key that opens the door to power, because it lets people change the thoughts, actions, and decisions of other people. Influence isn't just about being able to control or manipulate people. It's also about being able to inspire and persuade people to join you in a cause or vision. Throughout history, powerful people have used their charisma, their persuasive speeches, and their magnetic personalities to get and stay in power. From Martin Luther King Jr. to Mahatma Gandhi, these people showed how having power can change the direction of a country.

To gain more influence, you need to know a lot about how people think and the art of persuasion. It requires building trust, gaining credibility, and mastering the delicate dance of social dynamics. Influence is the key to having power. It can come from the power of one's words, the strength of one's ideas, or the force of one's personality.

The Law of Authority:

The Law of Authority is the second law of power. Power is built on authority, because authority shows that a person or institution is legitimate and credible. Authority can come from many different places, such as knowledge in a certain field, a position or title, or even the power of tradition and social norms. It's important to show confidence, competence, and reliability if you want to be seen as a leader.

But authority isn't just about being recognized by other people; it's a state of mind. True authority comes from being very sure of yourself and knowing how to use your skills and abilities well. It is earned by doing things the same way over and over and sticking to your principles. Those who really have power are the ones who make people trust, admire, and respect them.

The Law of Strategy:

The Law of Strategy is the third law of power. Power isn't just won through brute force; it's also won through careful planning, strategic thinking, and a good understanding of the terrain. The Law of Strategy says that it's important to plan ahead, to think about possible problems and challenges, and to change your plan based on what's happening.

Strategic thinking is a mix of planning ahead, being creative, and being open to change. It requires the ability to see patterns, weigh risks and benefits, and come up with a plan that will give you the best chance of success. Strategic thinking is the key to getting things done, whether it's through analyzing the competition, researching the market, or planning for different possible outcomes.

The Law of Adaptation:

The Law of Adaptation is the fourth law of power. In a world where power is always shifting, the only way to stay alive is to be able to change with it. Those who don't change will be left behind as the changing tides of life take away their power. To adapt, you have to be willing to let go of old ways of thinking and acting and be open to new ideas and changes.

To adapt well, you need to be flexible, strong, and able to think ahead. It requires being able to spot new trends, predict future problems, and change one's approach to meet those needs. Those who can adapt are the ones who do well, whether they are business leaders who change their companies or politicians who change with the times.

The Law of Perception:

The Law of Perception is the fifth law of power. Power, like everything else, is shaped by how people see it. How people see you is one of the most important factors in getting and using power. It's not enough to have power; you also have to be seen as powerful. The Law of Perception shows how important it is to control and change how other people see us.

Some ways to control how people see you are to build a strong personal brand, create an air of mystery, and tell a story that shows off your power and authority. Symbols, visual cues, and strategic communication can all be used to change how people see things. The powerful have a lot of ways to change how people see them, from politicians who carefully stage-manage their public image to business leaders who create a culture of prestige and exclusivity.

The Law of Control:

The Law of Control is the sixth law of power. To use power well, you must have control over yourself. Discipline and self-awareness are needed to control emotions, impulses, and actions. Lack of control can lead to making hasty decisions, acting erratically, and losing power.

Gaining and keeping control requires a deep understanding of oneself, mastery of one's emotions, and a commitment to self-discipline. Self-reflection, mindfulness practices, and forming healthy habits are all ways to gain control. When you learn to control yourself, you become a force that can't be ignored.

By understanding the Laws of Power, we can see how power works and how it changes over time. Whether we want power for personal gain or to make the world a better place, the Laws of Power show us how to get there.

The Ethics of Power

In the world of power, there is an unspoken but underlying expectation that people will act in an ethical way. The idea of power ethics means that people have a responsibility to use power in a way that takes into account the moral implications and possible outcomes of their actions. It's an admission that power can have positive and negative impacts.

However, the conflict between power and ethics can be extremely complicated. Power can be addicting, making it tempting to break moral rules for personal gain or to use other people to get what you want. When you are in a position of power, it can be very hard to stick to your morals. This requires constant self-reflection and a commitment to being ethical.

We can learn about the potential for ethical power by looking at the actions of people who have used power well while staying true to ethical principles. These case studies not only show the good things that can happen when power is used ethically, but they also give others ideas about how to use power in a constructive way.

On the other hand, unethical power can have terrible effects. When power is used without regard for moral principles, it can hurt both individuals and society as a whole. Abuse of power can lead to social injustices, violations of human rights, and widespread suffering. The consequences of unethical power serve as a reminder that it is morally important to always think about the ethical implications of what you do.

It is very important for people in power to make decisions that are ethical. It requires careful thought about the results of choices and how they might affect other people. To deal with moral dilemmas, you need to have a strong moral compass and be willing to put the well-being of those affected by your decisions first. People in power must always ask themselves why they do what they do and be accountable for how they use their power.

One of the most complicated things about power is that it can change the values and priorities of an individual. Power has the ability to change people, which often makes them reevaluate their morals. This kind of self-reflection is important to avoid corruption and keep a sense of morality and fairness when in power.

Power Dynamics in History

Power dynamics have been a big part of how historical events and societies have changed over time. From ancient civilizations to modern democracies, power has been the driving force behind the rise and fall of empires, the fight for dominance, and the search for justice and the good of society.

When looking at the rise and fall of empires, it's clear that getting and using power have been at the center of their paths. Leaders and the ruling classes have used many different ways to get and keep power, such as military conquest, political alliances, and economic dominance. These shifts in power within empires have also affected how they relate to other countries, which has changed the course of international relations and world events.

Power struggles between monarchs, priests, and military leaders were common in ancient societies like Egypt, Mesopotamia, and Greece. These differences in power played a big role in how the social, economic, and cultural aspects of these societies changed over time. Monarchs had complete control over the people, resources, and land, while priests had a say in religious matters. The military leaders also had a lot of power because they could keep order and protect the interests of the ruling class.

European powers exploited and controlled indigenous populations during the colonial and imperial eras. This use of power meant putting down native cultures, taking advantage of resources, and setting up oppressive regimes. Even now, the effects of colonialism are still being felt in the political, social, and economic systems of the countries that were colonized.

Throughout history, revolutionary movements have tried to change the way power is held. Revolutionaries try to get rid of those in power in different ways. They do this because they don't like being oppressed or treated unfairly. These revolutions have had long-lasting effects on how societies have grown and changed, and they have sometimes led to new power structures.

Wars and other conflicts have also been caused by struggles for power. Inequalities in power and competition for resources often lead to violent fights.

These wars have effects that go far beyond the battlefield. They change societies and the way the world works.

In modern democracies, the way power is distributed is shaped by how political parties, interest groups, and the media work together. To keep a balance of power, you must understand how these things work. But this balance isn't always stable, and the difficulties and complexities of giving and using power can lead to corruption and abuse.

Case studies of historical events can be very helpful in understanding how power works. By looking at specific cases like the Roman Empire, the French Revolution, and the Civil Rights Movement, we can learn lessons that can be used in a wider range of situations to understand how power works.

Power dynamics have left an indelible mark on history, shaping both people and nations. When you have power, you need to think about ethics, and you need to think about yourself to avoid corruption and keep a sense of morality and fairness. For ethical power dynamics to work, there must be accountability, transparency, and checks and balances. To promote ethical power dynamics, it's important to be aware of social differences and give people the knowledge and skills they need to make decisions. Also, ethical power is not fixed; it must change over time to keep up with changing moral standards.

Chapter Two

Mastering Personal Power

Self-Awareness and Personal Power

Self-awareness is a powerful tool that lets us get in touch with our deepest selves and realize our full potential. It is the key to getting to know ourselves better and making the most of our strengths to gain more power. Without knowing ourselves, we might stumble through life, not knowing what we can and can't do. But if we work on becoming more self-aware, we can start a journey of empowerment and change that will give us personal power in all parts of our lives.

Self-awareness begins with self-reflection. We can learn more about ourselves by looking inward and examining our thoughts, feelings, and actions. When we give ourselves time for quiet thought, we go deep into our minds and find the hidden truths about who we are. Through self-reflection, we can unravel the layers that hide our true selves and make room for personal growth and self-actualization.

Finding out our own strengths and weaknesses is an important part of becoming self-aware and powerful. By figuring out what our strengths are and making the most of them, we can use them as powerful tools for success and fulfillment. Our strengths make us who we are and shape the unique things we can bring to the world. On the other hand, knowing our weaknesses lets us see and work on areas where we need to improve. We can get a clear picture of our strengths and weaknesses by doing self-assessment exercises and asking others for honest feedback. This gives us the power to move through life with purpose and intention. In-depth information about the various self-assessment tests available are covered in the book 50 Shades of Personality.

Self-confidence goes hand in hand with self-awareness and personal power. We can find and get rid of insecurities and self-doubt by getting to know ourselves better and exploring our inner landscape. The journey of self-awareness gives us the tools we need to build a positive image of ourselves. This gives us the confidence to be our true selves. We can build a strong foundation of self-confidence that shines from the inside out through positive self-talk, visualization, and celebrating our past successes.

Self-acceptance is a key part of personal power. By accepting our strengths and weaknesses without judging them, we can be authentic and have more influence. When we fully accept ourselves, we can use our unique qualities and face life with a sense of inner wholeness and alignment. We can cultivate a mindset of self-acceptance by practicing self-compassion and reframing negative self-perceptions. This will allow us to step into our power with grace and authenticity.

Personal power is heavily reliant on emotional intelligence. By becoming more self-aware of our emotions and getting better at managing them, we can increase our personal power and deal with other people in an effortless manner. Mindfulness practices and empathy exercises can help us develop our emotional intelligence and respond to others with compassion, understanding, and grace. By using our emotional intelligence, we can harness the power of our emotions, making our relationships healthier and giving us more success in all areas of life.

Personal power requires nurturing and self-care. We can identify and address our physical, emotional, and mental needs through self-awareness, ensuring that we are operating from a place of strength and vitality. Putting rest and relaxation first, setting limits, and asking for help are all important parts of self-care. By making self-care a part of our daily lives, we strengthen our personal power and set ourselves up for success and well-being.

The journey toward self-awareness and personal power is an ongoing one that requires dedication, patience, and a willingness to explore the depths of our being. But with each step, we get closer to finding out what our true potential is and embracing the wide range of personal power we all have.

Building Confidence and Charisma

Building confidence and charisma are critical steps in harnessing personal power. These traits have the power to captivate and inspire others, gaining attention and influence. Throughout history, important people have been successful because they were sure of themselves and had a lot of charm. From charismatic leaders like Martin Luther King Jr., who inspired a movement with his strong presence and unwavering belief in his cause, to influential entrepreneurs like Oprah Winfrey, whose charisma captivated millions, confidence and charisma have proven to be powerful tools in the pursuit of power and influence.

Developing self-assurance is the first step to building confidence and charisma. It requires a deep look at oneself and the building of a good image of oneself. People can boost their confidence and get rid of self-doubt by having positive self-talk and doing visualization exercises. Self-assurance grows even more when people leave their comfort zones and take on new challenges. A big part of being charismatic is believing in oneself and projecting an air of self-assurance.

Developing charisma involves more than just looking good. It means using your body language, voice tone, and overall demeanor to get people's attention. People who are charismatic are able to connect with others on an emotional level by showing empathy and being great listeners. Because of these qualities, they can get genuine individuals to follow them and build strong relationships. Examples of charismatic leaders, like Winston Churchill and Malala Yousafzai, show the effect that these traits can have on those around them.

Both confidence and charisma depend on being able to communicate well. To inspire others, you need to listen carefully, speak clearly, and be able to explain your ideas well. The ability of storytelling to captivate an audience and inspire action should not be underestimated. People who are charismatic know that good communication can help them get people's attention, get their message across, and get them working toward a common goal.

Both confidence and charisma are built on authenticity. To build trust and get closer to other people, it's important to be true to yourself and show your real feelings and values. Embracing authenticity lets people gain true followers and build a strong personal brand that other people can relate to.

Building confidence and charisma depends a lot on building rapport. To connect with other people, you can use techniques like mirroring their body language, actively listening, and finding things you have in common. The power of rapport comes from its ability to build trust, bring people together, and get people to pay attention. By getting better at building relationships, people improve their ability to persuade and lead others.

In conclusion, building confidence and charisma is a multi-step process that requires self-awareness, continuous learning, and the cultivation of authenticity. These traits have the power to captivate and inspire others, gaining attention and power.

Emotional Intelligence and Power

Emotional intelligence is a key part of power dynamics because it shows how well a person can understand and control their own emotions and the emotions of others. It is important in many parts of life, such as personal relationships and the workplace.

Emotional intelligence gives people the tools they need to understand and control their own emotions. Self-awareness and self-control are important parts of emotional intelligence because they help people understand and manage their emotions. When people have this level of self-awareness, they can handle power dynamics with more confidence and control because they can respond in a calm and strategic way.

People who have a lot of emotional intelligence, for example, can use their emotions to their advantage when it comes to power dynamics. They can recognize the emotions they're having and use them in a way that helps them reach their goals. They can use their anger to get them to do something about an injustice, or they can use their compassion to make connections and inspire others. They have a greater sense of personal power because they are in tune with their emotions.

Emotional intelligence is a key part of being a good leader and managing people well. Leaders with a lot of emotional intelligence can inspire and motivate their teams by being aware of and understanding the emotions of others. They can create an atmosphere of trust and psychological safety where people feel valued and heard. This positive power dynamic makes the team or organization more productive and helps people work together.

In the same way, emotional intelligence is a big part of negotiating and solving conflicts. People with a lot of emotional intelligence can understand and deal with the emotions of others in these situations. By understanding how the other side feels, they can find common ground and work toward solutions that are good for both sides. This ability to deal with different kinds of emotions leads to good solutions and a fair distribution of power.

In conclusion, emotional intelligence is a powerful tool for understanding and navigating power dynamics. It gives people power by helping them understand and deal with their own emotions and emotions of others. By working on and improving their emotional intelligence, people can use all of their personal power and do well in many areas of life.

The Power of Mindset

There are times in life when challenges seem insurmountable, failure seems unavoidable, and our dreams appear distant and unattainable. But in the midst of these challenges is the power of mindset, a strong force that can change our reality and help us get where we want to go. The key to this power is learning how to think positively.

When we have a positive mindset, we can get past the limits that other things put on us and reach our full potential. When we have a positive attitude, we can see problems as chances to grow and transformation. We don't let problems get us down because we have a strong belief in our abilities and an optimistic attitude that pushes us to think of new ways to solve them.

History is full of stories about people who used the power of positive thinking to overcome challenges that at first seemed impossible to overcome. Take the well-known Thomas Edison as an example. Even though he failed many times in his search for the incandescent light bulb, he never stopped believing in himself. He said at one time, "I haven't failed. "I've just found 10,000 ways that won't work." He overcame problems by keeping a positive mindset. When he finally finished his groundbreaking invention, he lit up the world with the power of his positive attitude.

Positive thinking is the key to success, but limiting beliefs are like chains that stop us from moving forward. These are the deeply rooted ideas and beliefs that hold us back and stop us from reaching our goals. To use the full power of mindset, it is important to find and challenge these limits you put on yourself.

We can gradually dismantle the walls erected by our limiting beliefs by reframing our negative thoughts and seeking alternative perspectives. Think about the story of Oprah Winfrey, who overcame a rough childhood and went against what society expected of her to become one of the most influential people of our time. By changing from a victim mentality to one of empowerment, she was able to reach her full potential and build an empire that continues to inspire and help millions.

Beyond positive thinking and challenging limiting beliefs lies the concept of growth mindset. Carol Dweck, a psychologist, came up with the term "growth mindset." This is the idea that our skills and intelligence can be improved through hard work and dedication. Adopting this way of thinking makes us love learning and be willing to take on challenges, which leads us to success.

People who have a growth mindset are more resilient, motivated, and able to change. When things don't go as planned, they see it as an opportunity to learn and grow. They don't shy away from challenges; instead, they dive right into the middle of them. They know that embracing the unknown is the best way to get out of a rut.

Think about the story of Elon Musk, a visionary entrepreneur who started companies like Tesla and SpaceX. Musk never gave up on his goal of changing the automotive and aerospace industries, even though he had many failures and setbacks along the way. He once said, "Failure is an option here. If things are not failing, you are not innovating enough." By developing this way of thinking, he was able to turn setbacks into stepping stones and, in the end, achieve extraordinary success.

When it comes to mastering your mind, the power of visualizing and setting goals is a powerful driver. By clearly picturing how we want things to turn out and setting clear, realizable goals, we can use the huge power of our minds to make our dreams come true.

When we visualize our goals, we create a blueprint that guides our actions and decisions toward achieving them. Visualization keeps us on track and keeps us motivated, just like a compass keeps a ship going in the right direction. By making SMART goals—goals that are specific, measurable, achievable, relevant, and time-bound—we can turn our dreams into real milestones that we can use to track our progress and change our course if we need to.

Consider the story of Serena Williams, the legendary tennis player who has broken records and redefined greatness over the course of her career. Williams always visualized herself standing on the winner's podium after winning a major tournament, even when she was very young. She used the power of her mind to become one of the best athletes of all time. She did this by setting clear goals and constantly seeing herself winning.

In the pursuit of success, mental toughness is an unwavering pillar of strength. A big part of reaching our goals is being able to deal with problems, overcome obstacles, and keep going even when things aren't clear.

To be mentally tough, we need to have a positive outlook, take care of ourselves, and ask for help from others. Keeping a positive attitude helps us ride the unpredictability of life's waves with grace and resilience, turning obstacles into stepping stones. Taking care of our mental and physical health gives us more energy and helps us face problems with clarity and strength. Also, asking for help from mentors, friends, and loved ones gives us a network of encouragement and advice that helps us keep our minds strong and makes us more determined.

Think about how well-known author J.K. Rowling had to deal with a lot of rejections and financial problems before the world loved her Harry Potter series. Despite her despair, she forged ahead with unwavering mental toughness, believing in her creative vision and refusing to give up. Her persistence and ability to bounce back from hard times helped her reach the top of the literary world.

Fear is a strong emotion that we all feel, and it often slows us down and stops our natural drive to grow. To fully use the power of mindset, you have to go through the dangerous terrain of fear and come out on the other side victorious.

To get over fear, you need the right amount of courage and risk-taking. Courage gives us the strength to face our fears head-on and refuse to let them paralyze us. This courage gives us the confidence to face the unknown, take calculated risks, and keep going after our dreams no matter what.

Think about the story of Malala Yousafzai, a Pakistani activist who stood up to the oppressive Taliban regime to fight for girls' education. Even though she was threatened with death and violence, she didn't give in to fear. Instead, she stood up for the rights of millions of girls around the world. She used the power of her mind to become a symbol of hope and inspiration by getting over her fears and taking risks.

When we face problems that seem impossible to solve, persistence is a steady force that keeps us moving toward our goals. The power of mindset is based on this unwavering commitment and determination to keep going, even when things look bad.

By working on being persistent, we build up the strength to weather storms, turn setbacks into stepping stones, and, in the end, control our own lives. We keep moving forward, inch by inch, even when the odds are against us, because we don't give up. Dreams come true when people work hard to make them happen.

Think about the story of Nelson Mandela, who was a beacon of hope and, after 27 years in prison, became a symbol of forgiveness and reconciliation. His unwavering determination in the face of oppression and hardship led to big changes in society and helped end apartheid in South Africa. Mandela's legacy shows us that hard work and an unstoppable attitude can change not only our lives but also the world around us.

In the end, keep in mind that we all have the power to change our minds. It is a power that wants to be used, a source of strength that wants to be tapped. When we use the power of positive thinking, challenge our limiting beliefs, develop a growth mindset, keep going no matter what, and practice mindfulness and self-reflection, we take control of our own lives. We build our own power and paint the world with bright strokes of purpose and impact.

Chapter Three

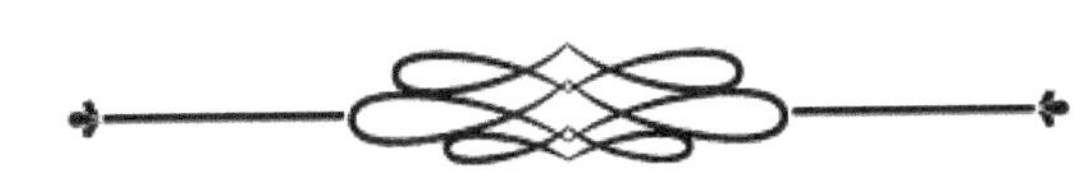

Manipulation and Persuasion

As I dug deeper into the subject of psychological manipulation techniques, I discovered myself on a treacherous path. It was a place where power was king, and those who knew how to use these strategies had a big advantage. This knowledge was important not only for self-preservation but also for figuring out the complex web of power dynamics and control that permeated every part of our lives.

Power of persuasion was the first technique that caught my attention. It had become an art form after being changed for hundreds of years. Those who were good at psychological manipulation found it easy to win people over by using logic, emotion, and social proof. People didn't know it, but these techniques were slowly shaping their thoughts and actions, like a potter shaping clay.

I learned that psychological manipulation is based on playing on people's emotions. Fear-mongering, making us feel guilty, and love-bombing were just some of the ways we were made to feel a certain way. These strategies took advantage of our weaknesses by pulling on the strings of our hearts until we were nothing but puppets dancing to the manipulator's tune. It was scary to realize that emotions we thought were real and personal could be manufactured and manipulated with such skill for control.

But gaslighting was the most dangerous method of all. It was a psychological attack on a person's sense of reality, a twisted dance of lies meant to make the victim question whether or not they were crazy. Gaslighting turned people's lives into whirlwinds of confusion and self-doubt, chipping away at the truth until it was hard to tell what was real and what wasn't. I was both fascinated and repulsed by how powerful this technique was, since it went after the very core of a person's identity.

Psychological manipulation relied heavily on power dynamics. Manipulators used dominance and submission, preyed on insecurities, and undermined others' confidence to maintain control, whether in personal or professional relationships. By understanding how these power dynamics work, I started to see the cracks in the facade of manipulation.

Psychological manipulation went beyond personal relationships and into the wider world. Media and propaganda became the main ways to change people's minds and control the stories they told. Propaganda techniques like spreading false information, playing on people's emotions, and framing were used on a large scale to slowly change how whole nations thought. It was a shocking reminder that even the truth could be skewed if it was presented in the right way.

Psychological manipulation was woven together with lies and words that were meant to trick people. Lies, half-truths, and patterns of persuasion were carefully chosen to trick and sway people. This dishonest communication had an effect that went beyond just words. It got deep into our minds, clouded our judgment, and led us astray.

As I came to the end of my research, I couldn't help but notice how common psychological manipulation techniques are in everyday life. They were hidden in the marketing messages that we were constantly exposed to, in the political rhetoric that shaped our views of the world, and in the subtle ways that power played out in our relationships. It was a stark reminder of how important it is to be aware and think critically when dealing with manipulation.

Armed with this knowledge, I made a promise to take charge of my own story, resist the pull of manipulation, and teach others how to do the same. For in the shadows of manipulation was the chance for real freedom, where the different shades of power turned into a kaleidoscope of strength and authenticity.

Body Language and Nonverbal Communication

To really understand the art of power and control, you have to explore the complicated world of body language and nonverbal communication. These silent ways of expressing have a huge impact on how people interact with each other. They let us send messages and manipulate others in a very subtle way. Body language goes beyond what words can say and shows more about a person's intentions, emotions, and desires than words alone. As I learn more about how power works, it's becoming clear that learning the secrets of body language is one of the most important things I can do to get a grasp on how power works.

One of the most important aspects of body language is our facial expressions. The human face is an intricate canvas that can easily show a wide range of emotions, from happiness to sadness, anger to fear. With just a smile, a furrowed brow, or a narrowed gaze, we can silently show how we feel and what we want. When we understand the link between facial expressions and emotions, we can not only figure out how other people really feel, but also use their emotions to our advantage. The face is a window into the soul, and those who are capable to understand its complicated language can learn a lot from it.

In the world of nonverbal communication, the way we move and stand also sends important messages. Each action, whether done on purpose or unintentionally, sends a unique message. Crossed arms can be a sign of resistance or defensiveness, while open palms show trust and honesty. A person's posture also says a lot about how confident, dominant, or submissive they are. By changing our gestures and postures on purpose, we can change the balance of power in a room and have control and influence without saying a word. The trick is to master the art of intentional body language, in which every move is made for a specific reason.

People often say that the eyes are the windows to the soul because they can tell a lot about a person without them saying a word. Eye contact is very important because it can show trust, interest, or dominance. Keeping steady eye contact can give a sense of authority and dominance, which can subtly change how others see our power. It is important to note, however, that the interpretation of eye contact differs across cultures, with some societies viewing direct eye contact as disrespectful or confrontational. So, one must know how to navigate this delicate dance of gazes and make sure that their intentions are understood and accepted.

Distance and proximity reveal unspoken messages in personal space. Proxemics, the study of how people relate to each other in space, is a key part of nonverbal communication. Whether it is the intimate closeness of lovers or the deliberate distancing of rivals, the manipulation of personal space is a powerful tool in establishing power dynamics. By getting into or getting out of someone's personal space, we subtly show them that we are dominant or submissive, which affects how we interact with them. When we understand and use proxemics well, we can use the ebb and flow of power to our advantage.

As you learn about the different kinds of power, it becomes clear that nonverbal cues are powerful tools that can be used to control and manipulate people. Every action we make on purpose or unintentionally sends a message to the people around us, which affects how they see and react to us. By learning the subtleties of body language, we can influence and control other people whenever we want. When used strategically, these silent cues give us a powerful way to exert our will and get the results we want.

To really understand how powerful body language is, you have to practice and use it. Theoretical knowledge alone isn't enough to get a deep understanding of nonverbal communication. It needs to be combined with real-world experience. By putting ourselves in real-life situations and paying attention to and analyzing body language, we can catch skilled manipulators or become influential people. By applying our knowledge into action and mastering these attributes, we unlock our potential to use our power and navigate the complicated dance of human interaction.

When I think about how important body language and nonverbal communication are in understanding shades of power, I am left with an unwavering conviction. The study of these silent but powerful cues reveals a world where actions speak louder than words, where intentions are whispered in body language, and where power is used to control the invisible thread of unspoken messages.

Chapter Four

Power in Relationships

In the complex realm of intimate relationships, power struggles can creep up like shadows, weaving their way into the very fabric of the connection between two souls. Power, which is a strong force, can show up in these intimate spaces in different ways, such as through control, manipulation, or dominance. Power struggles can be very bad for a relationship because they can leave emotional scars and upset the delicate balance of trust and mutual respect between the individuals involved in it.

When you try to figure out where power struggles in close relationships come from, you find a tangled web of unresolved conflicts, different expectations, and broken communication. Power imbalances grow in the cracks of these long-standing problems because they thrive on the uncertainty and vulnerability in the relationship. When problems aren't solved, they fester like open wounds, leading to power struggles that are fueled by the need to be in charge.

Gender roles and social expectations make power struggles in romantic relationships even more complicated. Societal norms that have been around for a long time act like puppeteers, pulling the strings that control how men and women share power. Often, traditional gender roles, expectations, and stereotypes determine how power is shared, which leads to endless fights for control and dominance. When this happens, the desire for power is a distorted sign of the pressures of society.

People use many different ways to gain control in close relationships when they want to be in charge. Emotional manipulation, making the other person feel guilty, and even sneaky methods like "gaslighting" are used as weapons to break the other person's will and gain control in the never-ending power struggle. Each carefully planned move brings the relationship deeper into the darkness, suffocating the light of love and compassion.

When people in close relationships are stuck in a never-ending cycle of power struggles, it has serious effects on their emotional and mental health. The constant fight for control wears on a person's sense of self-worth, as every setback and loss chips away at their sense of self-worth. As power struggles spread their long, dark shadows over every part of life, happiness seems like a distant memory.

Even when things look the worst, there is still hope that things will get better. To talk about and solve power struggles in close relationships, you have to be brave enough to look inside yourself and be willing to talk openly and honestly. These are the ways that people can come to an agreement and learn to respect each other's boundaries. When power struggles are solved, the power of vulnerability and empathy shines through as the foundation for a better relationship.

But it's important to know that power differences can grow into something more dangerous and harmful. In abusive relationships, there is a dangerous imbalance of power that can lead to verbal, emotional, or even physical abuse. It's important to know how to spot the signs of an unhealthy or abusive relationship and to get help and support from people who know how to get through this dangerous terrain.

If power struggles in close relationships aren't resolved, they can have long-term effects that hurt the very core of the relationship between the two people. Trust, intimacy, and the overall health of the relationship are all hurt, which could cause the union to break up or even end. The stakes are high, and if power struggles aren't dealt with, they can be very bad.

Contrary to what you might think, power struggles can help close relationships change and grow. Even though conflict is hard and often hurtful, it can be a chance to grow as a person and in your relationships. People learn how to navigate the murky waters of power in these situations, coming out of them with more maturity, understanding, and resilience.

Seeking professional help or counseling can be a light in the dark for people who are in power struggles. Couples therapy or relationship coaching provide a safe place to talk about and fix the problems at the root of power imbalances. People can heal wounds and change the way power works with the help of a trained professional. This makes relationships healthier and more fair.

As people go through life and build relationships, they must constantly think about themselves and grow. When given the chance, power struggles tend to happen again and again. People can change by using the lessons they've learned from the past to create better power dynamics in their future relationships. Through this commitment to growth and self-awareness, the chains of power struggles can be broken, and love can grow in its purest form.

In the middle of power struggles, there are the seeds of change. To get through these dangerous waters, you need courage, the willingness to be vulnerable, and a strong desire to build a world where love isn't overshadowed by power, but where power is used to lift and nourish the human spirit.

Power Plays in the Workplace

In the competitive world of work, it's important to know how to deal with power dynamics if you want to move up in your career. The delicate balance of power at work can make or break a person's career. Power plays can give people a big advantage in their careers if they understand them and deal with them in a smart way.

Positioning yourself as the underdog can be a very effective way to gain power. By acting like the underdog, people can get their coworkers and bosses to feel empathy for them and help them out. To play the underdog card well, you need to be vulnerable, humble, and know how to move strategically. For example, telling personal stories about struggles and how you overcame them can make people feel connected to you and help you get support. But it's important to find a good balance, because too much playing the role of the underdog can backfire and be seen as manipulative. The key is to show your strengths and accomplishments in a real way while subtly bringing up the problems you faced along the way.

Having strong personal relationships at work is a powerful way to move up in your career. People can get a lot out of networking and forming partnerships with important people. To build these relationships, you have to do more than just talk to people on the surface level. You have to put in time and effort to make real connections. By helping others, working together on projects, and looking for a mentor, people can build a network that will help them understand how power works and open doors to new opportunities. It's important to treat these relationships with honesty and be ready to help each other out when needed.

Power Balancing in Relationships

Achieving and maintaining power balance is an important part of all human relationships, no matter how complicated they are. It's a complicated dance between two people, a delicate balance that needs to be cared for and kept up. If you don't do anything about it, power dynamics can ruin even the best relationships, leaving behind anger and unmet needs.

Power balance in relationships is more than just a surface issue; it affects every aspect of how people interact with each other. When there is an imbalance of power, one person has too much control over another, making the other person feel weak and helpless. This unfair arrangement will eventually destroy the relationship, planting the seeds of anger and discontent.

Take the case of Sarah and Mark, who are deeply in love but have a problem with power. As a result of her strong and assertive personality, Sarah always dominated Mark, making him feel weak and unimportant. As the gap between them grew, their once-loving relationship slowly turned into a fight over unmet needs and unspoken anger. The imbalance of power not only stopped people from growing as individuals, but it also stopped people from really getting close and connecting with each other.

There are many overt and covert ways that power imbalances show up in relationships, leaving behind hurt feelings and unrealized potential. When someone wants to get the other person to do what they want, control, manipulation, and dominance become the tools of choice. People who are brave enough to look below the surface can always see the signs, even if they aren't always clear.

Controlling someone is a common sign of an imbalance of power. One partner may always make choices without asking for input or taking into account what the other person wants and needs. It seems like their power comes from stifling any kind of independence or uniqueness.

Another sneaky sign of a power imbalance is manipulation. In reality, it's a way to stay ahead, even though it looks like acts of care and concern. The manipulator uses psychological tricks to change the other person's thoughts and actions in a way that benefits them. This kind of power difference makes people less trusting and more angry.

Lastly, dominance shows itself by stifling the other person's voice and power. The dominant partner might put down the other person's feelings and thoughts by saying they are not important or valid. People who are oppressed lose their sense of self-worth and confidence when they are in a situation where they don't have enough power.

An imbalance of power in a relationship has effects that go far beyond the two people involved. They get into everything that happens and poison the relationship at its core. Both people suffer because their personal development is stunted and their authentic selves are suffocated. A suffocating power dynamic takes the place of the chance for a loving and fulfilling relationship.

The Role of Communication in Power Balancing

Communication is the most important part of the complicated dance of power balance. Talking to each other openly and honestly is what moves the relationship forward and gives people hope when things aren't going well. Power differences can be dealt with, broken down, and turned into a symphony of equality and harmony through good communication.

Active listening, which is essential for good communication, needs focus and understanding. It means letting go of your own judgments and assumptions and making room for the other person to share their feelings and thoughts. To truly listen is to value the other person's voice and make it stronger with respect and understanding.

When two people feel empathy for each other, they can better understand what the other person is going through. It means putting yourself in the other person's place and feeling their happiness and sadness, their fears and hopes. Empathy not only makes it easier to talk to each other, but it also grows compassion, which gets rid of the artificial barriers that power differences create.

However, listening and understanding are not enough for communication to work well in power-balancing efforts. It requires being ready to give in and find common ground. When you go into a conflict with an open mind and a sincere desire to find a solution, it can become a chance to learn and grow. Actively negotiating and finding common ground can smooth out the rough edges of power differences, making a space where everyone feels heard and valued.

Chapter Five

The Dark Side of Power

Even the most honest people can become corrupted by power. It messes with their morals, bends their rules, and tempts them with the promise of unchecked power. Power can be very addicting, and people have done terrible crimes against humanity because of it. Many examples can be found in history. As examples, Adolf Hitler and Joseph Stalin used their power to commit horrible crimes and cause unimaginable suffering. This abuse of power not only taints the person involved, but it also leaves a permanent mark on history, a chilling reminder of how weak human virtue is.

In the dark corners of power lies an evil force that preys on the weak and controls them according to its own will. People in positions of power often take advantage of their control over those below them, using their power as a tool to manipulate and control others for their own benefit. There are many stories in the world about people who were abused by those in power, whether at work, in personal relationships, or in formal social structures. There are many ways that exploitation can show up, such as sexual exploitation that leaves victims scarred and without any sense of self-worth and economic exploitation that causes income inequality. It's a scary reminder that power can be used to oppress people if it's not checked.

Tyranny and oppression are the worst things that can happen when you have power. Throughout history, despots and dictators have taken pleasure in their power and used it to control whole groups of people and make them do what they want. From the cruel

Roman emperors who put down dissent and ruled by their whims to more modern examples like Saddam Hussein and his brutal regime in Iraq, the true nature of power is shown by its ability to control and oppress. These tyrants hide behind the illusion of doing the right thing because they are sure that their actions serve a higher purpose. However, the long-lasting damage they do to society shows how twisted and evil power can be when it's used by people who don't care about others.

A dangerously high concentration of power threatens the very foundations of democracy. When a small group of people have a lot of power, the system of checks and balances breaks down. This makes way for autocracy and the loss of the values that keep a society free and fair. Democracies have fallen apart in the past when leaders, high on power, took down the checks and balances that were supposed to stop abuses. During these times, democracy is on the verge of becoming despotism, which serves as a warning of how dangerous it is to let power get concentrated in the hands of a few dishonest people.

At its core, power wants to control and manipulate people. People who are skilled and malicious with it use methods that twist reality, change public opinion, and control people's thoughts and actions to further their own goals. Spreading false information like wildfire and using fear to stop people from speaking out becomes the main tool of the oppressor. Manipulators have the power to change society by blurring the truth and distorting realities. This is seen in the famous "weaponization" of media during fascist regimes and in modern-day manipulation through social media. These kinds of manipulation and control are used by people who want to stay in charge and keep their power.

When there are imbalances of power, systemic injustice continues, causing widespread inequality and pushing some groups to the edges of society. In the past, privilege has often been held by a small group of people, while the many have had to deal with oppression. Having big differences in wealth, opportunities, and access to basic resources shows the bad side of power. As a result, racism, gender inequality, and taking advantage of weak communities happen. People with power use it to keep things the way they are, which keeps the cycle of inequality going and makes it harder to achieve social justice.

It's rare for people who want power to leave nothing but destruction behind them. When people who aren't involved in power struggles get caught in the middle, they become pawns in a game they didn't sign up for. Power often hurts the people who don't deserve it the most, as wars, falling economies, and broken societies show. The dark side of power hurts people and communities in ways that are hard to heal. For example, families are forced to move because of conflict, and policies that are made without thinking are known to cause people to move. For those who want power, there is a price that must be paid, and it can change the course of their lives forever.

Power holds a strange attraction for people with certain personality traits, like moths to a flame. People who want to be in power are more likely to have traits like narcissism, Machiavellianism, and psychopathy. This tendency makes a poisonous mix where the need to be in charge and dominate comes before other people's needs and rights. The psychopath feels safe in the halls of power, where they can take advantage of and control others for their own benefit. Psychopathology and power working together in an unholy way is a very dangerous threat because it leads to abuse, corruption, and the loss of morals.

People in power often have to make sacrifices and compromises that are very hard on themselves in order to gain and keep power. Personal relationships can fall apart when people are busy with work and other obligations. As the lines between public and private become less clear, loneliness follows you around all the time. Making decisions, dealing with consequences, and being watched all the time can be hard on your mental health and well-being. People who have power often have to choose between duty and personal fulfillment, which means they have to make sacrifices. Not many people are willing to pay it, and even fewer fully understand it until they are stuck in the maze of power.

Even though power has a dark side, it is not an unbeatable force. Strategies and methods can be used to lessen the bad effects of power and make sure it is used for the greater good. Being accountable and open are the foundations of ethical leadership. We can lessen its destructive effects by setting up checks and balances, encouraging different points of view, and holding those in power to high moral standards. We can only protect ourselves from the abuses of power and change its course toward a more fair and just world if we all work together and stay alert.

Power is a complicated and multifaceted thing that needs to be carefully understood and negotiated. It has both good and bad sides. It can either raise the human spirit to great heights of kindness and success, or it can cast a dark shadow over society that brings pain and oppression. The bad side of power is a reminder of how it can be used to hurt people, steal from them, and be cruel. People need to pay attention to this warning and take action to make sure that power is used for good. By being aware of and fighting power's dark sides, we can make the world more fair and just, where power is a force for good instead of evil.

Chapter Six

50 Types of Power

Personal Power

I felt a sense of personal power growing in me as I sat there and took in the wisdom of the old teachings. Every part of my body felt like it was on fire from a dormant energy that had been woken up. At that moment, I realized that personal power wasn't something that happened to us or was given to us by other people. It was something that was already inside us, waiting to be released.

I learned that real personal power is more than just being strong or having a lot of stuff. Being able to draw on our own courage, strength, and determination is what it means. We need to be strong enough to accept our weaknesses and use them to help us grow. It's having faith in our own worthiness and the ability to handle life's challenges with grace and integrity.

First, I looked into different practices that would help me build my personal power and use it. I started meditating every day, and it helped me connect with the stillness of my mind and draw from its source of wisdom. Mindfulness helped me understand and control my feelings and thoughts by teaching me to notice them without judging them.

Working out became an important part of my journey because I learned that taking care of my body not only made it healthier, but it also made me stronger mentally and emotionally.

The most important thing I learned on my journey, though, was that personal power is not something that only one person can pursue. We are a collective force that gets stronger when we work together and help each other. I looked for people with similar interests and joined groups that encouraged growth and personal development. We made a place together where we could share our stories, get ideas from each other, and help each other through hard times.

I learned that having personal power doesn't mean controlling or dominating other people. Instead, it means giving yourself and those around you more strength. It's about seeing that everyone has value and potential on their own, and making the world a place where everyone can thrive.

When used correctly, personal power can change not only our own lives but also the lives of those around us. Still, it's important to remember that power can be very dangerous if it's not used properly.

Personal power should never be used to take advantage of or put down other people. Instead, it should be used to uplift and empower them. A big part of having personal power is treating other people with respect and kindness, even when you don't agree with them.

Also, having personal power means we have to actively listen and think about other points of view. Accepting different points of view and appreciating what others have to say leads to a more fair and inclusive use of power. As opposed to forcing or controlling others, the best way to bring about real change while respecting their individuality is to work together and cooperate.

Last but not least, personal power makes us accountable for our actions and forces us to learn from our mistakes. When we recognize and think about the effects of our power, we can grow and keep improving our moral compass. It's important to keep your personal power by being humble and willing to learn and change.

There will always be problems and setbacks on the path to personal power. With all of its uncertainties and complexities, life gives challenges that test our strength and determination. We can get through these problems, though, because we have personal power.

Remember that setbacks are not signs of failure; they are just steps you need to take to reach your goal. Accept the lessons you've learned from failure and see them as opportunities to grow. We can turn problems into opportunities for personal and professional growth if we use our personal power as a guide.

There is a natural link between personal power and personal happiness. We can be happy and fulfilled with our lives when we use our personal power in a way that is in line with our values, passions, and goals. Personal power is something we can develop and use to make our lives full of purpose, joy, and meaning.

Personal power gives us the ability to live our lives on our own terms and make decisions that are in line with who we really are. Developing different aspects of personal power, like self-discipline, self-confidence, and a growth mindset, helps us deal with problems, follow our dreams, and live our lives as they really are.

Accepting your own power will directly lead to living a meaningful life. There is something bigger than ourselves that we can contribute to when we use our personal power. When we align our personal power with a cause or mission that really speaks to us, we become positive change agents and find a lot of meaning and fulfillment in what we do.

In the end, having personal power gives us the freedom to live our lives the way we want to. It frees us from self-doubt, fear, and other people's expectations of us, letting us reach our full potential. Personal happiness is no longer a distant dream; it's a real thing that affects every part of our lives when we connect with our inner power and accept who we really are.

As this section on personal power comes to a close, I want you to think about what you've learned and use it in your everyday life. Accept your personal power, let your potential shine, and make your life full of meaning, joy, and goals that are met. You were born with personal power; claim it, use it authentically, and shine your unique brilliance into the world.

Expert Power

When someone is seen as an expert in a certain field, they have a lot of power and influence. This kind of expert power can be used in many areas of life, including work, personal relationships, and social interactions. Having the power to get people to respect you, make educated decisions, and follow your lead is a huge responsibility that you should not ignore.

It is very important to know what it means to be an expert. Knowing a lot isn't the only thing that makes someone an expert; there are other qualities and characteristics that make someone an expert as well. Expertise is made up of four main parts: knowledge, experience, skills, and competence. Our ability to stay on the cutting edge of our field comes from our constant desire to learn and grow.

It takes deliberate and dedicated work to become an expert. There are several steps to the process, and the first one is to pick an area and learn about what it involves. In this case, getting specialized education, training, and work experience are all necessary to fully understand the subject. Anyone who wants to become an expert should try every aspect, whether it's getting a degree, getting certifications, finding a mentor, or doing a lot of hands-on work.

The first step toward becoming an expert is to find and choose a field of specialization. It's about finding a way to connect our passion with our strengths and choosing a field where we can really shine. Exploration and thorough research help us find possible areas of expertise where we can make a big difference. To make the best decision, you need to pick a path that fits both your short- and long-term goals.

As soon as the area of expertise is known, the journey to gain more understanding and knowledge in that area begins. A desire to learn and broaden our horizons is needed. You can get specialized knowledge by doing things like reading, researching, going to conferences and workshops, and talking to people who work in your field. To become an expert, you have to keep learning throughout your life, looking for new ways to improve your knowledge in a world that is always changing.

Another important part of expert power is building credibility. It's not enough to know something; you have to show others that you know it. To build trust and credibility, people publish research papers, articles, or books, go to conferences and seminars, and share their knowledge by giving public speaking engagements. Credibility is based on being consistent and honest, which you gain over time by making important contributions to the field.

Experts are different from others because they know how to use their power well. It is very important to be able to communicate and come across as an expert. Sharing your knowledge must be an art that has an effect, whether you're in a professional setting like a meeting, an interview, or a presentation, or just talking to your coworkers and peers every day. It is important to learn how to share information in a way that interests and educates others.

Still, getting better at something doesn't come without problems and challenges. Many experts go through things like competing in a crowded field, dealing with skepticism, and feeling like they don't belong. To get past these problems, you need to be resilient, persistent, and able to adapt. These traits help experts find their way through the constantly changing fields they work in.

Expert power can be used by working together and connecting with other people. Sharing information and learning from each other's experiences can help people who are experts in the same field connect with each other and create an environment that encourages growth and development. Creating a strong professional network can lead to chances to work together and offer invaluable assistance on the path to becoming an expert.

Expert power comes with a lot of ethical responsibilities that should never be forgotten. Having a lot of power means having a lot of responsibility. It is important to always try to use your knowledge in an ethical way, for the greater good. A person who is ethical avoids doing things that aren't right, stays honest, and is aware of possible conflicts of interest.

To sum up, expert power is a force that has huge potential to change our lives. It's a lifelong process of getting better at what you do, using your knowledge in an honest way, and always trying to get better. We are going on this journey to improve not only our own lives but also the progress in the fields we have chosen. Let's enjoy the power that comes with being an expert and work to make a real difference with our knowledge and influence.

Coercive Power

Within the context of power, coercive power is the capacity to employ coercion, threats, or punishment to make people conform. When someone with coercive authority uses terror to inspire fear of undesirable outcomes—like harm or retaliation—when they issue demands, they are able to establish control.

Relationships where one party is in a position of dominance or authority over the other frequently exhibit this power dynamic. Coercive power may result in short-term cooperation, but it can have negative long-term impacts as well, such as fostering a culture of fear and submission.

It is necessary to examine the complexities of coercive power and differentiate it from other types of power in order to fully understand its nature. Coercive power feeds on fear, in contrast to legitimate or expert authority, which is based on respect, knowledge, and common values. It takes advantage of weaknesses and manipulates feelings to exert control. The psychological implications of coercive authority are deep for both the person using it and the person receiving it. Because they enjoy inciting fear and submission in others, those who possess the power to dominate and manipulate others may develop a sense of superiority and domination. But this can also cause individuals to see power in a distorted way, making them oblivious to the consequences of their actions. On the flip side, the recipient, caught in a fear-driven cycle of compliance, could feel worthless, anxious, and helpless.

In daily life, coercive power can be obtained in a variety of ways. Taking control of others and putting yourself in a position of authority is one effective strategy. This may occur in personal relationships when one person dominates the other or in hierarchical organizational structures where people have leadership roles. People who hold these positions are able to use coercion to enforce compliance. Developing a reputation for ruthlessness and a readiness to punish non-compliance are further requirements for acquiring coercive power. This instills terror in the air, discouraging others from confronting or defying the wielding.

One can use a variety of strategies to exert influence and coercive power on other people. Implicit and explicit threats are often used strategies to induce fear and encourage cooperation. Coercive measures to enforce compliance include the imposition of consequences or punishments as well as the withholding of opportunities or incentives. Blackmail, gaslighting, manipulation, physical or verbal abuse, and manipulation are some techniques used to erode the autonomy and agency of others. The goal of these strategies is to make the target feel less valuable and dependent on the person using them.

Everyday life is infused with coercive power, which frequently takes on subtle and complex forms. In the context of parenting, for example, parents may use coercive methods to get their kids to comply, like grounding them, denying them privileges, or even using physical force. Similar to this, people in managerial or leadership positions may use coercive power to manipulate and control subordinates; they do this by instilling fear of punishment or termination in order to get cooperation. Subtle forms of coercion, such as emotional manipulation that fosters fear and dependency, can also be seen in interpersonal relationships.

Individuals possess the agency and ability to oppose and subdue the influence of coercive power. Developing assertiveness and resilience within oneself is essential to fending off coercive approaches. Being assertive gives people the ability to express their wants, set boundaries, and fend off unwanted influence. Furthermore, getting help from dependable family members, friends, or professionals can help you navigate the challenges of coercive power. Regaining personal power begins with recognizing and accepting one's value, autonomy, and the freedom to choose without interference.

Coercive power has effects on wider society institutions as well as interpersonal interactions. For example, in the political sphere, authorities may employ coercive measures to quell criticism, restrict liberties, and hold onto power. In interactions with citizens, law enforcement may also utilize coercive force, which may result in abuses of authority. Organizations with hierarchical structures may foster a climate in which the use of force is accepted, fostering a climate of dread and silent obedience.

Coercive power is based on a complicated web of psychological mechanisms. Coercive techniques can incite fear, which in turn can activate cooperation and obedience by appealing to our basic survival instincts and the need to keep ourselves safe. Gradually, the recipient's feeling of autonomy and self-worth is undermined, which encourages dependence on the wielder for leadership and direction. The power imbalance that results from this psychological manipulation warps both parties' perceptions and actions. Recognizing the negative impacts of coercive power and working toward the development of healthier power dynamics require an understanding of these psychological dynamics.

It is clear from the discussion of coercive power that there are moral questions and possible negative effects associated with this type of power. It is a malevolent force that destroys good relationships, individuality, and trust. In order to mitigate the adverse consequences of coercive power, people ought to give precedence to fostering positive power dynamics that are based on mutual respect, agreement, and candid communication. We can work toward a more just and caring society by comprehending the psychological processes at work, identifying the minute details of coercion in daily situations, and advocating for the moral use of power.

Reward Power

A crucial component of interpersonal and organizational dynamics, reward power gives people the capacity to regulate rewards, which in turn influences and motivates others. It is extremely important since it appeals to everyone's basic needs for approval, safety, and fulfillment. Fundamentally, the concept of Reward Power involves using material or immaterial incentives to promote desired behaviors, skill enhancement, and results. This power can be used by anyone who has the key to the rewards that others pursue; it is not just reserved for those in official positions of leadership.

A wide range of rewards can be used in the context of reward power to encourage growth or elicit compliance. Tangible incentives that meet tangible demands and ambitions, like money, gifts, or promotions, act as external motivators. They boost people's commitment and loyalty by giving them a sense of security and fulfillment. Conversely, intangible incentives such as praise, recognition, or opportunities for individual or professional growth, appeal to internal drives. These incentives support people's psychological health by creating a sense of fulfillment and self-worth, which in turn gives them the confidence to succeed and perform at higher levels.

Building a reputation for consistency, fairness, and transparency in reward distribution is necessary to gain Reward Power. This means fostering an environment of acknowledgment and providing incentives for desired actions in both the personal and professional domains. Developing trusting bonds with powerful people—mentors, peers, or superiors, for example—can also lead to getting higher compensation. Another tactic is to become an expert in a certain field and market yourself as a great addition to the company or community. Because of the perceived scarcity this expertise produces, rewards that one can provide become more desirable.

In order to use Reward Power successfully, one must have a thorough understanding of motivation. There are two types of motivation: extrinsic and intrinsic. An individual's internal motivation stems from their ideals, interests, or sheer enjoyment of the activity at hand. On the other hand, extrinsic motivation depends on outside elements like status, incentives, or recognition. A power holder can access a potent source of motivated and self-directed activity from those they influence by matching rewards with people's intrinsic motivations or creating an atmosphere that fosters intrinsic motivation. "The Ultimate Book of Motivation" is a great resource that can assist you in gaining a deeper understanding of motivation.

To fully utilize Reward Power, a well-thought-out reward system must be created. This entails determining the precise actions, viewpoints, or results that support one's aims and objectives. It's important to establish clear expectations so that people know what is expected of them in order to receive rewards. Incentives must to be relevant, distinctive, and catered to the particular interests and needs of the receivers. The person in charge can develop a strong sense of purpose and encourage a strong sense of loyalty, dedication, and engagement by matching rewards with each person's values and goals.

Utilizing Reward Power effectively requires careful consideration of timing and reinforcement. Rewarding positive behaviors in a timely and regular manner encourages their repetition. Strengthening the relationship between the power holder and the beneficiaries is achieved by positive reinforcement, which includes expressing gratitude, recognizing accomplishments, and celebrating milestones. However, since perceived injustice can cause demotivation and resentment, it is crucial to make sure that awards are viewed as just and equitable. A well-designed system of rewards and timely, regular reinforcement increases the influence of the power holder and lays the groundwork for loyalty and trust.

The moral implications of Reward Power are critical to consider. While using this type of power, those in positions of authority must put recipients' welfare, justice, and openness first. Unethical behaviors that weaken trust, incite animosity, and diminish the influence of those in positions of authority include favoritism, preferential treatment, and unfair reward distribution. It is crucial to make sure that incentives are given fairly and in accordance with merit in order to promote an atmosphere in which everyone has an equal chance to advance and be acknowledged.

A key component of reward power is acknowledging and appreciating others' accomplishments and contributions. A culture of recognition can be fostered by those in positions of authority to make people feel important, respected, and in control. This can be accomplished by giving thanks on a frequent basis, praising achievements, and setting up venues where people can share their triumphs. Powerful people encourage and urge those around them to realize their own potential by elevating others via acknowledgment. This not only increases their own impact.

To maximize influence and control, one must comprehend how reward power interacts with other types of power. One way to inspire people in a variety of ways is to combine Reward Power with Expert Power or Coercive Power. Reward Power combined with Expert Power, for example, can increase people's intrinsic motivation by associating incentives with competence and personal progress. Similarly, using Coercive Power in conjunction with Reward Power can instill fear or dire repercussions while rewarding cooperation. By examining these power relationships, those in positions of authority can strategically use Reward Power and modify it for various circumstances.

Referent Power

Referent power entices the minds and hearts of people who hold it; it is a captivating force that surpasses conventional kinds of authority. It is a power based on likeability, charisma, and the mysterious capacity to enthrall and inspire people. Referent power is based on respect and appreciation from other people, as opposed to the rewarding power of money rewards or the coercive power of fear. It's an illusive, ethereal energy that comes from deep within, enticing people into their orbit and demanding complete devotion. Referent power transforms into a magnetic force in a variety of social and professional settings, influencing other people's attitudes, feelings, and behaviors.

A thorough understanding of referent power requires delving into the incomprehensible depths of human psyche. Referent power is based on a foundation of trust, authenticity, and credibility. People that have referent power have an aura about them that connects with other people, making them feel drawn in by their sincerity and alluring presence. Their ability to negotiate the complex web of human relationships and establish meaningful connections that go beyond superficiality is a result of their high interpersonal skills and emotional intelligence.

Referent power is a skill that may be developed via self-awareness and personal development rather than being an inherent talent given onto a small number of people. In order to discover their true identities, those who want to use referent power must go on an introspective journey that involves exploring the deepest corners of their souls. People can create enduring and sincere connections with others by being vulnerable and accepting of who they are. Referent power thrives because of these relationships since they promote loyalty and trust, which strengthens their control over others.

Referent power's attraction is found in the charismatic traits held by its practitioners. They can fascinate and interest their audience by using expressive body language, excellent communication, and active listening. Even the hardest-to-win people can be won over with a sincere grin, a tender touch, or a skillfully constructed story. The way one looks, their self-assurance, and their narrative skills all contribute to the aura of mystery that surrounds persons with referent power.

Referent power gives leaders a special capacity for motivating and directing their followers. Instead of using force or authority to control others, they lead by establishing a model that other people want to follow. Leaders possessing referent power develop a positive company culture that stimulates growth, cooperation, and innovation by infusing their vision with unrelenting passion and sincerity. Their impact extends beyond hierarchical power, fostering a congruent match between the organization's objectives and its individuals' ambitions.

Referent power has a captivating quality that seeps into personal relationships and transcends the sphere of professional influence. Genuineness, empathy, and trust serve as the cornerstones of deep interactions that last throughout time. By exhibiting the characteristics that lead to referent power, people can develop influence and likeability in their interpersonal relationships. Their warmth attracts partners, their presence serves as a source of inspiration and strength, and friends seek their advice.

Continuous self-improvement and personal growth become the pillars of one's journey in order to preserve and sustain referent power. Others' confidence and loyalty would wither away without the authenticity that initially ignited this power, thus it must be zealously preserved. Referent power endures because of a person's everlasting dedication to personal progress and their commitment to staying true to themselves.

Referent power is an infinitely pervasive impact that permeates every aspect of daily life. People use social interactions as a platform to use their ability to constructively inspire, motivate, and influence others. Referent power can be used in work settings to foster harmonious teams, stimulate creativity, and establish unified cultures.

I feel incredibly empowered when I consider the path I have taken to explore the depths of referent power. I've evolved from being a passive witness of the dynamics of power to a master of my own fate, equipped with the knowledge and discernment to control this alluring force. I keep developing my charisma, making sincere relationships, and motivating those around me every day. Referent power's attraction has braided itself into my own being, irreversibly altering the course of my existence. I also bring the addictive charm of referent power with me as I walk out into the wide stretches of possibilities, prepared to make a lasting impression on the world.

Legitimate Power

It is important to understand that legitimate power, which is also known as positional power, is different from other types of power. People get it because of the roles and places they hold in different areas of their lives, such as at work, at home, or in society. People with legitimate power can influence others, make choices, and change the course of events because they have the authority and legitimacy to do so.

If someone is recognized and accepted for their rightful authority, that person has legitimate power. It comes from the idea that certain jobs or positions have power and deserve respect because of the rules and structures that are in place for them. To use legitimate power, you have to make sure that your actions and decisions are in line with the rules and standards that come with your position. When it comes to politics, organizations, and connections, legitimate power can look different, but its basic principles stay the same.

Authority and legitimacy are two very important parts of power dynamics. It's what real power is built on. People who are subject to authority know and accept it. This is called legitimacy. This is what gives people in power the right to make decisions, impose rules, and lead others. Legitimate power is useless and loses its meaning without acceptance of authority and the legitimacy that comes with it.

There are many legitimate sources of power, and each one gives a person's authority a different quality. People who have official jobs in a company, like executives, managers, or team leads, have the legal right to direct and influence the people who work for them. In the same way, elected leaders in political systems get their power from the mandate that the people give them. Social norms and cultural practices also play a part in the sources of legitimate power, putting some people or groups in places of authority and influence.

Different from other kinds of power, legitimate power has certain traits that make it legitimate. It comes from the formal frameworks and roles that exist in a certain setting. When someone has legal power, others recognize and accept their authority. This is different from coercive power, which is based on fear and punishment, and reward power, which is based on rewards. The legitimacy that comes with the position makes it easy to make decisions, allocate resources, and lead others.

The way other people see legitimate power is a key factor in how well it works. When people think that people in power are fair, just, and knowledgeable, it makes their power seem more legitimate. On the other hand, legitimate power may meet challenges and resistance if it is seen as unfair, arbitrary, or not competent. What followers or subordinates think affects the balance of power in relationships, organizations, and societies. This is why people in power need to work hard to build trust and confidence.

To get real power, you need to plan and think things through. People can increase their legitimate power in both personal and professional situations by becoming more credible and trustworthy. Building a strong base for genuine power requires being consistent in what you do, being able to communicate clearly, and having a strong work ethic. People can become respected and influential by making sure their values and actions match what is expected of them in their jobs.

Informational Power

Informational power is a type of power that is very important but not always thought of. You get it by having and sharing useful information, and it's very important in both your personal and professional lives. In a world that depends more and more on information, being able to find and use information well can mean the difference between success and failure. Giving people the information and insight they need to make informed decisions and take meaningful action gives them informational power, which gives them authority and influence over others.

Having informational power means being able to control and influence other people by having and sharing useful information. It's not enough to just know things; you also need to know how to use and share that information in a way that gives others power. Information that gives you this kind of power can come from many places, like research, business knowledge, market trends, or new ideas. When used correctly, informational power gives people the ability to change results, lead conversations, and make decisions that are in line with their own interests and goals.

To gain informational power, you have to make a conscious effort to keep learning, keep up with the newest trends and news, and actively look for information that can be useful in certain situations.

It is a journey of curiosity and discovery that lasts a lifetime, driven by a sincere desire to learn more and share useful insights. Being dedicated, intellectually curious, and determined to stay ahead of the curve in your field are all things that will help you gain informational power.

Credibility and Informational Power go hand in hand. Not only does someone need to know a lot, they also need to build an image for being reliable, accurate, and trustworthy. To build credibility, you should always give well-researched and well-documented information, cite reliable sources, and show your knowledge through accomplishments and successes. People who have Informational Power should also be ready to listen to others and admit when they don't know something. They should also always try to be intellectually honest.

Individuals must learn how to successfully use their Informational Power once they have it. One way to get the most out of Informational Power is to share what you know with others. People can establish themselves as reliable advisors and information sources in their networks by becoming the go-to source for information. They can also use information in a planned way to affect outcomes and decisions, guiding conversations in a way that fits with their values and goals.

It's important to get and use Informational Power for your own benefit, but it's also important to give this kind of power to other people. Sharing information and knowledge with others helps people learn and grow all the time. Building a network of people who can pool their information to benefit the whole makes it feasible to effect positive change on a bigger scale. Give people informational power, and it will help them individually and also make the community or the organization smarter and more knowledgeable as a whole.

Connection Power

Connection Power is the skill of being able to make and keep real, important connections with people, at work and in your personal life. Being able to connect deeply with other people can help you grow, find opportunities, and gain influence. Connection power is an important part of success and influence that is often ignored in personal development. Making and keeping connections is important for creating long-lasting relationships that can help us reach our goals, motivate us, and give us the support and direction we need.

There are different kinds of connections, such as personal, professional, and social ones. Personal relationships are those made with loved ones, family, and close friends. These relationships give us a sense of support and belonging in our daily lives. People in our business, workplace, or career field make professional connections. Making these connections is important for getting ahead in your career, developing your skills, and finding fresh opportunities. Social connections include more than just our friends, coworkers, and people who share our interests and hobbies. These connections can help us see things from different perspectives, work together, and make our personal and professional lives better. To get the most out of Connection Power, you need to keep a network of connections in all of these different areas.

Trust, mutual respect, and a real interest in others are what make relationships real. Being real and sincere with other people is important if we want to make real relationships with them. We need to be present in conversations, listen attentively, and show that we can empathize. Being open and vulnerable, letting others see our true selves, is also a part of making real relationships. Being honest with other people builds trust and a connection, which are the building blocks of good relationships.

Making relationships is only the beginning; it's also important to care for and keep them over time. To keep connections strong, we need to talk to each other often, show respect, and help each other out when we can. This could be as easy as sending a caring message, checking in on them, or letting them know you're proud of what they've done. Regularly connecting with others helps to strengthen the bonds we've made and makes sure that those connections stay strong and important.

One of the best things about Connection Power is that it lets us use our relationships to find opportunities. Having a lot of connections makes it more likely that we'll find new opportunities, whether it's through introductions, suggestions, or working together. To use connections well, you need to know what other people want and need and look for ways to help and add value. When we truly care about other people and look for ways to help them, we build a relationship that works for both.

Connection Power isn't bound to a single network; it can grow and change. We need to actively seek out new opportunities to grow our network and increase our Connection Power. For example, we could go to networking events, join industry groups, or use online platforms for connection building. By always looking for new connections, we open ourselves up to new ideas and improve our chances of meeting like-minded people who can make our personal and professional lives better.

Resource Power

Resource power is the ability to manage and control others by having and using valuable things, whether they are tangible or not. Resources can be things like money, land, or technology, or they can be ideas, skills, or connections that can't be seen or touched. Having these resources and knowing how to use them well gives people a clear edge, giving them the tools they need to reach their goals and realize their dreams.

Finding and using our own resources is the most important thing we can do to gain Resource Power. Realizing the riches that are inside us, whether they are physical or not, and knowing how to use them to reach our full potential is the first step. Like a digger looking for valuable gems, we need to dig deep inside ourselves to find the many resources that are there waiting to be found.

Getting money is an important part of Resource Power because it helps us figure out how to get around in our complicated world. There are a lot of ways to get rich, from smartly saving and spending to starting your own business or moving up in your current job. But it's important to remember that getting money isn't an end in itself; it's a way to improve our power and control. Knowing how to handle money and being good with money are important for getting the most out of these resources and making sure they stay a source of power.

Financial means alone are not enough, though. When it comes to getting Resource Power, intellectual resources are very valuable. You can buy things with your mind, and the key to growth and power is to keep learning. To get intellectual tools, it's important to keep learning new things, pick up new skills, and stay up to date on what's going on in your field.

The search for information gives us power, giving us the confidence and skills to take charge of our own lives and the lives of others. This is true whether we get it through formal education, training programs, self-study, or networking.

Making use of Resource Power isn't limited to one area of life; it affects every part of our lives. People who are resourceful can change and control events in their daily lives by making good use of their resources. They can change the topic of conversation, change people's minds, and make things happen in their favor. But it is very important that the way Resource Power is used is moral. As the saying goes, "With great power comes great responsibility." To use Resource Power in an ethical way, you must use it to help yourself and others, make things better, and encourage everyone to get along.

There will, in fact, be problems along the way to getting and using Resource Power. Problems may include not having enough money, friends, or other things that get in the way. Still, these problems can be faced and solved with unwavering drive. To get around these problems, people can do a lot of different things, from coming up with creative answers to making new friends. Our best tools for getting past the problems we face on our way to Resource Power are persistence, toughness, and the flexibility to change to new situations.

Finally, I want everyone reading this to think about their own resources and how they can be used to get and use Resource Power. The first step in the journey is to become aware of all the tools we have, both tangible and intangible. By working hard to get financial, intellectual, and social resources, we give ourselves the power to change and manage our situations. We can get through our personal and professional lives by being ethical and strategic. This will help us reach success, happiness, and eventually a life powered by Resource Power.

Positional Power

Positional power is a big part of how people deal with each other. It can be found in social structures, organizational hierarchies, and even personal relationships. It's a force that gets stronger based on your position or part in these structures; it acts as a channel for power, control, and influence.

There are many ways to get to positions of authority and impact within the huge field of positional power. Leadership roles, management roles, and positions of power in many different areas come together to form a constellation of power that lights the way. People who are lucky enough to be in these roles are in charge and can use their power to successfully guide, shape, and change the world around them. They have the power to use the combined strengths of people, groups, and organizations to guide them toward common goals and objectives.

Power in a position is appealing because it can bring many benefits to the person who has it. Making decisions becomes their tool of choice because they have the power to decide what to do in crucial situations. Their power earns them respect and admiration, which makes both coworkers and subordinates pay attention and follow them. When someone has positional power, they can also change people's minds, affect outcomes, and change the direction of organizations or social structures. Still, there is a heavy load hidden in the cracks of these benefits. Each decision is weighed against responsibility and accountability, and the chance of misusing or abusing power is always there, ready to taint the good goals of those in charge.

Getting positional power is a hard process that requires persistence, drive, and a well-thought-out plan for your job. Getting to higher places in your career requires moving up the career ladder, getting the right qualifications and skills, and building a strong network. These tactics are backed up by stories of trailblazers who carefully planned their ascent and had huge successes along the way. These people show that consistent hard work, unwavering drive, and the guts to face problems head-on can lead to the highest level of positional power.

When you have a lot of power, you need to be careful not to give in to the temptations of control and abuse. It's important to find a delicate balance because positional power can cause problems and make teams and groups toxic. In these rough seas, it's important to learn how to fight and balance positional power. Positional power can be used in a more collaborative and welcoming way by asking for different points of view, encouraging feedback, and giving others the freedom to challenge authority. This is better than letting it run wild, which can lead to problems.

Under the smooth surface of positional power, there are many problems and dangers waiting to be discovered. As people rise in power and influence, these problems will appear, trying their character and ability. It's hard to keep power and humility in check when ego and hubris are around to ruin the good goals behind positional power. People's skills at navigating the rough waters of workplace politics are put to the test when conflicts of interest arise. People have to be careful because of the complicated web of power dynamics in teams and groups. They have to be aware of the delicate balance between leadership and empathy.

Getting positional power shouldn't be the end of your journey; it should be the start of a long journey of growth and development. To stay significant and make your power more useful, you need to be committed to ongoing learning, skill development, and keeping up with changes and trends in your field. People who really understand the possibility of their positional power are always changing, adapting, and striving for excellence.

Emotional Power

Emotional power is more powerful than mental or physical strength alone. It's a power that lives in the depths of our feelings and is woven into our very being. Before you can fully grasp the idea of emotional power, you need to know what emotional intelligence means. To have emotional power, we need to be able to recognize, understand, and manage our own emotional states as well as the emotions of others. Emotional intelligence helps us understand how people interact with each other, which gives us the tools to make connections, settle disagreements, and influence other people. It's the base on which emotional power is built.

It's not a single feeling that gives you power; it's a mix of different emotions. Our emotional power comes from all of our feelings, including happiness, anger, sadness, and fear. In order to use our emotional power to its fullest, we need to understand and manage these emotions. We need to learn to understand the different shades of each emotion and accept them without letting them control us. By understanding and managing our emotions, we can use them as tools instead of letting them run our lives.

Being aware of and managing your emotions are two important parts of emotional power. Self-awareness helps us understand our emotions, abilities, and weaknesses in a clear way. It is the most important thing we can do to improve our emotional intelligence. Self-regulation helps us learn to handle and moderate our emotional responses, so we can choose how to respond consciously and purposefully. Knowing ourselves and being able to control our emotions help us handle our feelings with grace and poise, which increases our emotional power.

But emotional power is not something that exists by itself. Emotional power is all about making emotional bonds with other people. One important part of making these links is empathy, which means being able to understand and share someone else's feelings. Strong relationships are built on emotional connection, which makes it possible for trust, kindness, and understanding to grow. We can't say enough about how powerful empathy and emotional connection are. They allow us to change people's minds, make the world a better place, and affect others.

You don't have to be in the business world to have emotional power. It affects every connection and interaction we have in our personal lives as well. When it comes to our daily lives, emotional power helps us make deep connections, deal with the difficulties of love and closeness, and grow as people and improve ourselves. Using our emotional power can make our relationships happier, more peaceful, and more fulfilling. It can also help us feel good about ourselves and build our inner strength.

When it comes to work, emotional power is a key factor in success. It helps us deal with the complexities of the workplace, put together strong teams, and lead with kindness and integrity. We can communicate clearly, inspire and motivate others, and make sound decisions when we have emotional power and a deep understanding of others' emotions and needs. We can be successful in our careers, make the workplace a better place to be, and leave a long impression on the companies we work for by using our emotional power at work.

There will always be conflict in your personal and work life. However, it is during times of disagreement and conflict that emotional power really shines. When there is a disagreement, emotional power gives us the tools to relate to and understand the other person, ease emotions, and find a solution. As a result, we can have tough talks, handle our feelings well, and turn disagreements into chances to grow and make peace.

We need to put self-care first if we want to keep and build up our emotional health. Self-care is not a nice-to-have, it's a must for our emotional well-being. Setting limits, being kind to ourselves, and doing things that make us happy and recharge are all parts of it. By putting self-care first, we fill up our emotional tanks, which lets us be completely and authentically be present in every part of our lives.

While we learn more about emotional power, we must also be aware of how it can be abused. Emotional influence is an adverse component of emotional power that is used to take advantage of and control other people. By learning about emotional intelligence and emotional power, we can spot and avoid misleading tactics.

Emotional power is not a fixed quality; it is a skill that can be improved and made stronger. We can grow and improve our emotional power by using tactics that we can put into action and doing exercises. Some of these tactics are practicing mindfulness, writing in a journal, going to therapy or coaching, and thinking about yourself. Emotional intelligence and emotional power can be fully developed with constant effort and practice.

As this study of emotional power comes to a close, I am struck by how powerful it is and how it can change things. Emotional power is not something to be afraid of; it's something to accept and use in a good way. In both our personal and professional lives, it is an important tool that helps us build relationships, deal with problems, and make positive changes. We can use our emotional power to its fullest and create a life full of authenticity, happiness, and deep connections if we are self-aware, empathetic, and dedicated to ongoing growth and development.

Cultural Power

In our society and the world as a whole, cultural power has a profound impact. Cultural power is the ability to change the rules, views, values, and behaviors of a group of people. It can be used by people, groups, and institutions, and it has the power to change the course of history.

Cultural power has roots that go all the way back to the beginning of society. The ancient Egyptians used art and architecture to shape their society, and the Renaissance thinkers used their ideas to change the world. Cultural power has always been a part of the human experience. It shows what our group consciousness is like and how it affects how we think, see, and affect the world around us.

Depending on where it comes from, cultural power can come from many different areas. Culture gives people power, and it can come from their knowledge in a certain area, like writing, science, or the arts. Having power in cultural institutions like the media or the school system can also come from their involvement in those domains. Additionally, people who are able to influence and arrange public opinion through activism or advocacy can have a lot of cultural power.

A big part of how society is made is cultural power. It makes and supports dominating stories, which control public debate and opinion. It has an effect on politics and society, changing the rules and laws that control our lives. Over the course of history, cultural power has been used to change society norms and values, whether it was to fight for racial or gender equality or social justice.

But there are some moral issues that come up with cultural power. As people who have cultural power, we need to be aware of problems like misrepresentation and cultural appropriation. We need to make sure that how we use cultural power is moral and ethical, and that we reflect different cultures and communities in a respectful manner.

The ways that cultural power works have changed in the digital age. Digital platforms, social media, and digital influencers have become strong ways to change national norms and values. The power of these platforms can now be used by individuals to share their own cultural views and question dominant narratives, making culture more open and diverse.

But cultural power is really strong when people work together and do things as a group. By working together, people and groups can make their views heard and change things in society more effectively.

Getting cultural power and using it well isn't always easy. People who want to gain and use cultural power may face big problems like systemic injustice, exclusion, and resistance to change. To deal with these problems, some ideas are to find and break down oppressive systems, build alliances and connections, and disrupt the status quo.

Political Power

At the heart of every political system is the concept of political power, which means having the ability to shape and control the political processes and institutions that affect society. It includes the power and authority that people and groups have to make decisions, enforce laws, and run the country. But people who are elected or hold places of authority are not the only ones with political power. It's not just formal positions; it also includes the informal power that important people and interest groups have over political outcomes.

Being able to shape and direct the institutions and processes that run society is what political power is all about. People who are part of the force decide what laws are made, who gets to speak, and how resources are shared. Politicians are in charge of making decisions and can change the direction of a country.

Power in politics affects people's lives by making laws that affect their ability to get health care, go to school, and find work. It decides how resources should be used and how law systems should work. The decisions that people in power make have huge effects on the lives and ways of making a living of ordinary people.

Political power can show up in a lot of different ways, from the official to the casual. Formal power is often held by people in government places of authority, whether they were elected or were given their jobs. These people have the legal and institutional power to make choices and follow through with plans. Power, on the other hand, is not limited only by the formal frameworks of government.

Informal power, which is held by powerful people and interest groups, can have a big effect on how politics turn out. Lobbyists put pressure on people who make decisions to support policies that benefit them. People with a lot of power in the media and academics can change public opinion, which can have an effect on political discourse. In political systems, power dynamics include both formal authority and the informal impact that people and groups have.

There are many places where political power comes from, and each one adds to the legitimacy and impact of the person who has it. People have known for a long time that wealth and economic means can give people a lot of political power. Rich people can get access to chances, special treatment, and networks that give them an unfair advantage in power.

Power can also come from your social standing and reputation. Individuals with a high social standing are more likely to be trusted and have a say in how decisions are made. Expertise and knowledge can also be used to gain political power, since people with specific knowledge are often sought after for help and direction.

Building networks and connection with powerful people and interest groups is a common way to get political power. Politicians who are good at their jobs know how important it is to build coalitions and relationships that can help them gain more power and influence. They learn political skills like how to negotiate, communicate, and think strategically so they can get along in politics.

Economic Power

Economic power is more than just the acquisition of wealth or control over resources; it is a manifestation of influence, a driver of change, and a measure of personal and communal prowess. To understand what economic power is really about, you have to look past the appeal of money. In its simplest form, economic power means being able to control resources, money, and the way markets work. It goes beyond the personal and affects the building blocks of society and the direction of businesses.

The ways people get to economic power are as different as the people who take them. Some people use their entrepreneurial spirit to venture into uncharted business territory, while others seek the guidance of education and choose jobs that will provide them with financial security and the chance to move up. Putting money into yourself and into innovative projects is the way to get economic power.

When you get economic power, it stays with you for the rest of your life. It gives people the power to make crucial decisions, face obstacles with confidence, and create their own futures. It helps people reach their personal and business goals, gives people the building blocks for their dreams, and is the key that opens doors to success.

Economic power needs to be carefully managed to make sure it lasts and has an impact for a long time. It requires a strong base of financial planning, diversified investments, and thoughtful wealth management. By finding the right mix between growth and stability, economic power can stay a loyal friend instead of a cruel boss.

People who have a lot of economic power have a chance to use it for the good of everyone. Giving back to others becomes not only a chance, but also a requirement, as people use their money and other resources to help others and make society better. Businesses start to understand that they can make a difference for the better on a global and a local level through corporate social responsibility.

Getting rich isn't the only way to be powerful; giving others power is too. When economic power opens up chances for others, helps the economy grow, and encourages job creation, it becomes a force for change. When economic power gives other people the tools they need to grow and thrive, it changes society as a whole.

That being said, economic power does come with some problems and limits. People with economic power are always at risk because the economy is unstable, markets are volatile, and power can be abused. It takes toughness, the ability to change, and a deep understanding of the fine line between using power wisely and giving in to its allure.

It is important to remember that economic power can change the world in deep and long-lasting ways. Anyone who wants to get through the complicated web of economic power needs to learn how to understand its subtleties, use its potential, and do so in a responsible way. As we continue on our journey through the fifty shades of power, let us remember the transformational potential of economic power and the enormous impact it can have on our lives and the world we inhabit.

Moral Power

Of all the different types of power, moral power is one of the most important. It means being able to influence and lead others through moral behavior and ideals. It goes beyond authority and makes people honor and admire you more deeply. People often think of power in terms of control and authority. Moral power, on the other hand, is like a lighthouse that points people in the direction of a higher goal.

Moral power is different from other types of power because it is based on honesty, ethics, and following moral rules. Instead of being based on fear or trickery, it is based on faith and credibility. Coercive power uses fear and penalties, and reward power uses rewards. Moral power, on the other hand, uses people's natural goodness and sense of what is right and wrong.

There are many things that make up the basis of moral power. Trustworthiness is the most important thing because it's what relationships and power are built on. Moral power has weight and conviction because it is based on credibility, which is gained by consistently acting in a way that is moral. Empathy, or being able to understand and share another person's feelings, makes it possible to build strong, real relationships. The last thing is that a strong moral sense acts as a guide, showing people how to handle tough moral and ethical situations.

Getting moral power takes a lifetime of self-reflection, personal growth, and learning from people who are moral role models. It takes a strong desire to keep improving yourself and a never-ending search for clarity on your ideals and beliefs. Having a strong sense of integrity and taking responsibility for your actions are essential if you want to gain moral power.

There are many threats to moral power because people's ideals can be tested and they may be pushed to break their integrity. People can get through these problems and keep their moral power, though, if they are strong and committed to moral ideals. Knowing yourself and thinking about what you believe are strong qualities that can help you deal with moral problems and stay true to your values.

To get around in the complicated world of influence, you need to find a balance between moral power and other kinds of power. Even though moral power is important, people must also be aware of and use other types of power, like positional or informational power, in order to do their jobs well. Understanding how these different types of power affect each other over time is important for taking a well-rounded approach that looks out for the greater good.

At the end of the day, moral power is something that goes beyond personal and work life. It's a power that you get, shape, and polish over time. This kind of power can change lives and determine futures if it is used correctly. As we talk about the different kinds of power, let's not forget how important moral power is and how it makes us responsible to lead with ethics and encourage others to do the same.

Charismatic Power

The key to both personal and professional success is charismatic power, which is a fascinating and magnetic force that comes from within. It is a power that goes beyond normal ways of influencing people and grips their hearts and thoughts.

Charm and authenticity are two of the most important parts of charismatic power. They can draw people in and inspire and influence their minds. It's a power that comes from an aura, a unique quality that can't be explained. A person with charismatic power has a lot of different traits and qualities, like self-confidence, charm, and the ability to connect deeply with others. It's an immeasurable force that is hard to teach but can be grown and improved.

Charm is built on self-confidence and self-assurance. Self-confidence and self-assurance are the buildings blocks of charming power. I think about how important it is to believe in yourself and be able to give off an aura of confidence, because it's this inner conviction that draws people in.

However, charm isn't just being sure of yourself. It requires developing a magnetic personality and charm, something that makes people want to be around us. Another important part of attractive power is the ability to connect with people and build relationships that matter. It takes us to learn how to actively listen and show that we understand, care about, and are interested in other people. But most importantly, we can use all of our charismatic power when we are authentic and passionate, when we show who we really are and let our interests guide us.

It may seem like charismatic power is a natural trait that only a few people are born with, but it can be built and improved by anyone. One of the aspects of having charismatic power is to understand the subtleties of nonverbal communication and learn how small things like body language and face expressions can make us more charismatic. Besides that, learn how to use storytelling and emotional connection to their full potential, understanding that they can captivate and motivate others. Mastering charisma is something that you do for the rest of your life, whether you're giving speeches, giving talks, or just talking to people in everyday life.

The real power of charisma shows up when we use it skillfully to persuade and affect others. To use charismatic influence effectively, you need to build your confidence and trustworthiness. People with great power can make the world a better place by setting a good example, building trust, and promoting a culture of authenticity and integrity. It also includes the art of inspiring and motivating others, looking at how to make a compelling vision and get people to join you in pursuing it. Also, knowing how to negotiate and solve conflicts well and how charm can be used to make situations where everyone wins, keep relationships peaceful, and encourage teamwork.

No path to charismatic power is smooth. It has its share of problems and difficulties. Getting over self-doubt and building self-confidence are two common things that get in the way of growing and acquiring this powerful force. How to deal with social anxiety and fear of being rejected, knowing that the ability to get back up after a failure makes you strong and resilient.

At this point in my research into the fifty shades of power, I have come to realize that the idea of charismatic leadership goes far further than I had imagined. It's helped me understand and learn more about myself, and it's taken me on a journey that changed me in ways that go beyond success and impact.

Social Power

To really understand what social power is all about, you need to look at all of its different forms and expressions. I began a journey to figure out how this force works by exploring the depths of power relations in social situations. Every type of social power shows a different side of it, from coercive power, which is based on fear and pressure, to referent power, which is based on respect and admiration. I look at the subtleties of how power shows up in communities, organizations, and relationships, knowing that it's a multifaceted force that can do good and bad things.

Building self-confidence, being true to yourself, and having a strong appearance can help your social power grow. I is also important to learn new things, improve your communication skills, and create a strong personal brand, since all of these can greatly increase your social power.

The strength of your social networks and relationships is an important part of your social power. It is important to make relationships that matter because relationships are what give people power. Social networks can be a strong tool for achieving personal and group goals by making real connections and giving and receiving help. It is also important for these social networks to be diverse and welcoming, because that means having different points of view that can increase social power in many ways.

When it comes to the complicated world of social power, social status is a big deal. Constantly improving oneself is a key part of rising in social standing. This includes everything from personal grooming and looking better to learning new things and getting better at things you already know. Making a name for yourself as a useful and recognized person can help you deal with power issues better.

A study of social power would be incomplete without a close examination of how it works in leading positions. It is essential to know how to take advantage of leadership opportunities, knowing that good leaders use charisma, influence, and emotional intelligence to get people to work together toward a common goal. Understanding how power works in a leadership framework helps find the best ways to encourage teamwork, independence, and success for everyone.

When it comes resolving conflicts, social power shows up as a strong force that can be used to get things done. Social power and conflict affect each other, knowing that power relations can make conflicts worse or better. Solve problems and make relationships better by using social power to help people understand, care about, and find common ground.

Social power changes everything about our lives, including our relationships, the decisions we make, and the world around us. Social power is not inherently good or bad; it is a tool that can be used to make yourself successful or to help others. Knowing about social power helps us deal with power issues, build relationships that include everyone, and push for change. We can change ourselves and the world by using social power in an ethical and accountable way. This will also make a permanent difference in other people's lives.

Network Power

Network power has become a significant concept in today's connected world, where connections are becoming more and more important for success. Network power means being able to use professional contacts, social networks, and online platforms to find opportunities, resources, and information.

To understand what network power is all about, you need to look at its parts and how they work together. The most powerful parts of a network are its social networks, which are made up of friends, family, and other people you know. They are the ones who can offer help, advice, and access to different opportunities. On the other hand, professional connections are what let you move up in your work, find new jobs, and find a mentor. Lastly, social networking sites like LinkedIn and X (formerly known as Twitter) have changed the way people network by letting them connect with other workers around the world who share their interests.

Strategy, intent, and authenticity are all important parts of building a strong network. Both in-person and online networking events give you an opportunity to meet new people and make connections. There are also many ways to network on online platforms, such as joining groups that are specific to your business and having meaningful discussions. But it's not just the number of links that matter; it's also how good they are. Building a strong network that will last for a long time requires building relationships based on trust, loyalty, and shared interests.

It doesn't matter how strong your network is if you don't know how to use it well. Using your network means taking into consideration the people you know and the tools you have access to in order to find opportunities and useful information. This can include anything from job leads and information about the field to mentoring and working together on projects. But to use a network effectively, you need to find a good balance between giving and receiving. It means taking care of relationships, helping out when it's needed, and being honest about your goals. People who use the network's power can open doors that would have stayed locked otherwise.

There are certain things you should and shouldn't do when you're networking. To make a good impact, you need to communicate clearly both in person and online. Maintaining relationships requires following up with people after the first meeting, showing gratitude, and staying in touch on a regular basis. On the other hand, it's just as important to know your limits, not bother people too much, and act professionally at all times. Following proper networking etiquette is essential for making links that last and getting the most out of your network.

A network isn't something that stays the same; it's always changing. Active reinforcement and growth are needed to make sure it lasts and is still useful. Going to events connected to your profession or interests is a great way to meet new people, share your interests, and make connections. Joining professional groups and associations can help you network with other professionals and give you access to useful tools and mentorship opportunities. For a network to grow over time, it's also important to stay linked and keep relationships alive through regular communication.

There is a lot of promise in building networks, but it's not always easy. Networking can be hard for people who are shy, short on time, afraid of being turned down, or have social anxiety. To get the most out of networks, though, you need to be aware of these problems and come up with ways to solve them. There are many ways to deal with these issues and build a network that fits your wants and goals, such as practicing self-confidence and having a growth mindset, getting help from mentors, and going to networking events for introverts.

Building and using a strong network based on important relationships can open doors, help you grow as a person, and bring about big changes. However, it is important to use network power with purpose, morality, and a desire to help everyone. We can make a difference in other people's lives and get through the complicated world we live in by using the power of relationships. People don't just think about network power; it's a force that, when used properly, can change our lives and help us succeed in every area.

Knowledge Power

It's true that knowledge is power. Over the course of history, people like intellectuals, philosophers, and leaders have said the same thing. But what does it really mean to have knowledge power? Knowledge power means being able to get, use, and apply knowledge and skills to improve your understanding, ability to make decisions, and total impact on the world. It's the secret tool that gives people the confidence and authority to handle life's challenges. This part goes into more detail about the idea of "knowledge power" and shows how important it is in everyday life.

Knowledge power is a unique kind of power that is different from conventional types of power like wealth or physical strength. Knowledge is something that goes beyond material things and social ranks because anyone who wants to learn can reach it. Although wealth and physical strength can be lost, the power that comes from knowledge lasts and grows with each new find.

Education is one of the most important ways to learn. It gives you the basic tools you need to understand the world, learn about different subjects, and improve your critical thinking abilities. People who go to school learn how to take in, analyze, and put together different pieces of information, which helps them make intelligent decisions. People can become powerful users of knowledge by opening the doors to the vast world of information through schooling.

Information is what gives knowledge its life. It's important to be able to tell the difference between useful and useless information in a world that is full of it. A skill that improves knowledge power is the ability to find reliable sources, think critically about what you read, and draw useful conclusions. When information is used correctly, it turns into a strategic asset that gives people the power to see trends coming, adjust to new situations, and change the outcome.

The spark that starts the journey to knowledge is curiosity. It's the never-ending desire to learn, ask questions, and discover. When people are curious and want to keep learning throughout their lives, they create a powerful combination that helps knowledge grow. Learning throughout one's life makes sure that information stays fresh and changes over time. This gives people the tools they need to adapt, grow, and do well in a world that is changing quickly.

Even though specialization is useful, knowledge is more powerful than that. Diversifying your knowledge helps you see things from different points of view, think about things from different fields, and solve problems better. People are able to approach difficult problems from different points of view when they learn about a wide range of topics. Diversifying information gives people the power to connect dots that don't seem to go together, which leads to innovation and creativity.

In the end, we looked at how education, knowledge, curiosity, expertise, and diversity can all work together to make a person smarter and more powerful. Knowledge power opens up a world of possibilities, and when we accept its potential, we also accept our own.

Perceptive Power

Discovering and controlling other people's power by knowing their thoughts, feelings, and plans is called perceptive power. It goes deeper than just talking to someone, letting people see what people are really thinking and feeling. By getting better at this skill, you can handle social situations, work settings, and personal relationships with more knowledge and the power to change things for the better.

A key part of perceptive power is emotional intelligence. It helps people understand and react correctly to other people's feelings. By working on their emotional intelligence, people can handle power dynamics better by knowing the deeper reasons behind others' actions and their weak spots. This knowledge gives them a clear edge in their interactions, letting them handle negotiations, leading roles, and making decisions with ease.

To improve your perceptive power, you need to work on certain skills. Active listening, observing, and keeping an open mind are all important ways to improve your ability to perceive. As long as people participate in conversations, really listen to what others are saying, and pay attention to facial cues, we can learn a lot about what other people are thinking and feeling. Being open-minded lets you see things from more points of view, which makes it easier to understand and connect with others.

A lot of perceptive power comes from nonverbal speech. An individual's body often says more than what words can express. People can figure out what other people are thinking and feeling by paying close attention to their body language, facial reactions, and other nonverbal cues. You can use this knowledge to change the way power works and get around it.

Trust is an important part of being observant. When people trust each other, they can learn even more about the thoughts, motives, and weaknesses of others. It makes people feel safe enough to say what they really think, which helps people with perceptive power get a better sense of the people they deal with.

But there is a bad side to being able to see things. Some people might abuse and change it to get what they want. People who have perceptive power should know that it is their moral duty to use it in a way that is responsible and shows respect for others. To keep things morally balanced, people must respect the autonomy and dignity of those they engage with.

There is a close connection between intuition and perceptive power. People with intuition can connect with their inner wisdom and gut feelings, which helps them understand other people better. People can improve their ability to correctly read and understand the thoughts and motivations of those around them by developing their intuition.

There are some problems and risks that come with having perceptive power. Biases, assumptions, and the chance of misunderstanding can make it hard to see things clearly. It is important to be aware of these possible problems and always work to reduce their impact. Self-reflection and meditation are important ways to deal with these problems and improve your ability to see things clearly.

To sum up, perceptive power is a powerful way to understand and change the way power works. People can deeply understand what other people are thinking, feeling, and wanting by developing empathy, emotional intelligence, and a range of perceptive skills. By using perceptive power in an ethical and accountable way, you can make stronger personal connections, have better work interactions, and grow as a person and as a group. Having perceptive power opens up a world of tools and enables handle the complicated world of human interactions with skill and impact.

Decision-making Power

Decision-making power is the ability to choose options and act, which affects the outcomes. It is the key to success.

The ability to think critically, solve problems, and analyze information are all necessary for making smart decisions. When we work on these skills, we can make better decisions that are in line with our values and goals.

It's also important to emphasize how important it is to carefully consider all of your options before making a decision. We need to think about the pros and cons of each option to make sure we make educated decisions. By thinking about all the options, we can make decisions that have the fewest risks and the most potential benefits.

Because we live in an unpredictable world, the ability to make decisions is even more important for getting through tough times.

How hard it is to make decisions when you need to balance short-term gains with long-term goals. In many cases, our short-term desires are at odds with our long-term goals. By knowing how the decisions we make affect our bigger goals, we can make sure that the decisions we make are in line with those goals.

Know that your intuition and gut thoughts can help you make decisions. Especially when we have to make tough decisions, our feelings can help us a lot. We can make better decisions when we trust and use our instincts and gut feelings well.

We all have biases that can make it hard to make good decisions. We can make more objective and rational decisions if we are aware of our biases and work to get rid of them.

It's not enough to be able to make decisions; we also need to know how to use that power. We can make the most of our decision-making power and get what we want by taking an organized approach and being flexible.

We have the power to make decisions about everything, from what to wear to big decisions that will affect our lives.

Real leaders know how important it is for everyone to be involved in making decisions and push others to do the same. It's important for creating an atmosphere where everyone's opinion is valued and taken into account when making decisions.

Inspirational Power

Inspirational power is a force that comes from inside us and lifts our spirits, pushing us forward on a path of growth, satisfaction, and impact. Inspirational power is a life-changing force that can affect all parts of our lives and help us reach new heights in our personal and professional lives.

Meditation, journaling, and being creative are all things that can help us awaken our dormant potential and use all of our inspirational power. However, inspirational power doesn't just live inside of us; it can also light a fire under those around us. Learn the art of inspiring and motivating others, including abilities and methods of doing things that give us the power to do that. You should definitely read The Ultimate

Book of Motivation. It goes into a lot of detail about the different things that motivate us and people around us.

Words have a lot of power; they can make you feel deep feelings and bring about big changes. It is very important to understand how language and speech affect people, to look into how carefully chosen words can inspire us and make other people passionate. From the eloquence of speeches to the power of writing, the art of using words has the power to change things.

Some leaders are naturally good at making people feel motivated and empowered, while others use different skills and methods. Some of the secrets of inspirational leadership are creating an engaging vision and making the workplace a place where people trust each other and work together.

We can change the course of our lives forever by following our inner calling, questioning the beliefs that hold us back, and starting a journey of constant self-improvement.

But big moments and amazing events aren't the only things that can inspire you. It's important to look for and find motivation in everyday things. We can add wonder and inspiration to our daily lives by becoming more aware and enjoying the beauty around us.

So many of us have trouble keeping our inspiration going over the long run. We can make sure that our inspiring flame stays bright by practicing self-care, looking for ways to keep learning and growing, and building a support system.

This amazing power of using stories to inspire and motivate people is what makes them so powerful. We will see how stories can evoke strong emotions, motivate people to take action, and shape our common consciousness, from myths and legends from the past to stories from the present.

Life is full of ups and downs, and you need to be resilient and persistent to get through them. Inspirational power helps us get through tough times and get back on our feet after a loss. We can get through any storm and come out stronger than ever if we believe in the power of resilience and work on being steadfastly persistent.

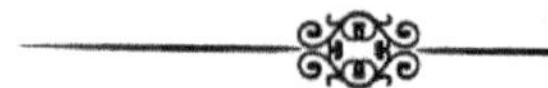

Persuasive Power

Before we can fully understand what persuasive power is, we need to look into the psychology behind it. Our thoughts are complicated and can be affected by many things, both consciously and unconsciously. These psychological processes are used in persuasion to show how complicated it is for people to make decisions and be motivated. By learning about the psychology behind persuasion, we can improve our ability to use words that get people to do what we want them to do.

Persuasion is not just an art; it is also a science, with a lot of study and theories that explain how it works. From the early work of social scientists to more recent research on the neuroscience of persuasion, the science of persuasion reveals how things work behind the scenes.

Different parts make up persuasive power, and each one is very important to how well it works. Persuasion starts with good communication, because being able to explain your points clearly and strongly can have a big effect on others. Another important factor is credibility, since people are more likely to agree with someone they trust and who seems knowledgeable. Emotional appeal is another part, since people aren't just logical beings but are also motivated by their emotions and desires. By breaking these down and understanding them, we can improve our ability to persuade and have the most effect.

Persuasion is based on trust, because people are more likely to follow someone they trust. To build trust, you need to know how important it is to be honest, trustworthy, and consistent. By building trust with others, we create an open and receptive space where our persuasive words can hit home and move people to take action.

There is no one right way to persuade someone; it's an art of making things fit the person. Different groups of people have different wants, needs, and points of view. Our persuasive tactics work better when we adapt them to fit these differences. We need to change our effective messages for each group of people, making sure that our words hit home and get the result we want.

When we try to convince someone of something, we often run into resistance to reasoning. It is profound to recognize and address objections to changing views and appealing to values. By doing this, we give ourselves the tools to deal with resistance and raise the chances of being persuaded.

Negotiation Power

When you negotiate, you need to be able to do a lot of different things well. It is the skill of navigating the tricky territory of getting what you want by negotiating and compromising well. Negotiation power isn't about dominance or force; it's about coming to agreements that are good for everyone and meet everyone's wants and interests. Negotiation power is an important skill to have in today's world, where disagreements often happen over ideas, resources, or goals. It helps us stand up for what we want, understand how others feel, and find things people agree on, which leads to good negotiations in the end.

Power in negotiations is different from standard types of power that depend on authority or control. It's a tricky skill that needs skill, strategy, and the ability to find middle ground. In negotiations, having power doesn't mean having the upper hand or being stronger than the other person. Understanding everyone's wants and needs and coming up with creative ideas that work for everyone is what it's all about. Negotiation power is about turning disagreements into chances to work together and come to deals where everyone is happy and willing to keep their end of the deal.

When people negotiate, their own personal power has a big impact on the result. Being confident, assertive, and self-aware are more important than having a job or title when it comes to personal power. It means being aware of and using your skills and unique qualities to improve your negotiation power.

One of the most important parts of negotiation power is doing a lot of research and preparation. It is important to understand the other side's goals, gather and analyze relevant information, and make a strategic plan before you start negotiating. By doing these things ahead of time, you can go into negotiations with confidence and a full understanding of the problems. When we are well-prepared, we can think of creative solutions to problems and make strong arguments that improve our negotiating power and the chances of getting good results.

Goals and objectives are very important when it comes to negotiating power. If you don't have clear goals in mind, negotiations can become pointless and useless. We can stay focused and put our energy toward getting what we want by making our goals clear and attainable. We can also figure out what is most important by ranking these goals, which helps us decide how to spend our time, money, and energy. This strategic approach gives us more negotiation power because it helps us make educated decisions, respond strategically to the other side's offers, and work toward results that are in our best interests.

Negotiation power is a skill that can be learned and improved by doing it often and analyzing it. It is an important tool for dealing with disagreements, finding answers that work for everyone, and making relationships stronger. Negotiation skills are useful in all areas of life because they help you successfully defend your interests, understand and relate to others, and come up with creative solutions that everyone can work on. I encourage you to learn how to negotiate as an important skill for everyday life because it can turn disagreements into opportunities for growth, success, and good relationships. Anyone can become a master of negotiation power if they work at it, practice, and are committed to doing it in an ethical and effective way.

Organizational Power

Organizational power is an invisible force that affects how an organization works, including its culture, how decisions are made, and its general success. It includes being able to persuade others, make decisions, allocate resources, and find your way through the complicated web of relationships at work. Understanding and using organizational power well is important for people who want to do well in their careers and move up in their fields.

There are different ways that organizational power can show up, and each has its own effects and traits. One type is formal authority, which comes from official positions or the way a group is set up hierarchically.

People who are officially in charge can make decisions, assign tasks, and set goals.

Another aspect of organizational power is resource control, which means being able to manage or distribute important resources within the company, like funds, staff, or equipment. People who have control over resources have a lot of power and can use it to change outcomes and rise in the company.

Another type of organizational power is decision-making power, which means having the power to make or change significant decisions. People who have the power to make decisions can change the way projects, initiatives, and the company as a whole go.

Getting organizational power is not a skill that you are born with, but one that you can develop by working at it. It's important to make connections and alliances because they can offer support, cooperation, and power within the organization. It takes time and effort to build relationships with coworkers, bosses, and subordinates. This helps us gain more power and see things from different points of view.

Another way to gain organizational power is to become an expert in something. Gaining a lot of information and skills in a certain area not only builds credibility, but also makes you an important resource for the company. We can have a bigger effect and have more power because we are always learning new things and keeping up with trends in our field.

In an organization, power challenges can come up in many ways, creating problems that must be solved in order to keep and use organizational power. For example, power battles can happen when people have different goals or are competing for resources or power. We can avoid power struggles and build bridges to cooperation by talking to each other in an open and constructive way, looking for solutions that work for everyone, and showing that we're ready to work together.

Another common power issue is being against change. People may not want to change, especially if it upsets the balance of power or threatens established standards. Build an atmosphere of open communication and participation to deal with this problem, and make sure that everyone has a say in the change process. We can get past pushback and power struggles that come with organizational change by actively listening to concerns, being honest about how we'll address them, and giving a clear reason for the change.

Conflicts can also weaken a group and slow down progress. Active listening, seeking common ground, and finding answers that are good for both sides are all good ways to deal with conflicts in a way that keeps relationships strong and moves both sides closer to their goals. We can get past the power problems that come up during conflicts and create a positive and productive work environment by keeping empathy and a focus on long-term teamwork.

Getting and keeping corporate power is an ongoing process that needs flexibility, initiative, and a strong network of support. It's important to keep an eye on how things are changing, both inside and outside the organization, and make changes to your strategies as needed. By constantly evaluating the organization's needs and goals, we can look for growth opportunities and position ourselves as a valuable asset.

Technological Power

In the present day; technology has become an undeniable force that affects how we live, work, and talk to each other. Understanding this idea is very important because it includes using technology to change the way things happen. People all over the world depend on technology more and more, and its effects on our lives are significant.

The ability to control and use technology to reach certain goals or results is one broad definition of technological power. It includes the information, skills, and tools that are needed to use technology well. Technological power is more than just having technology. It also means being able to understand, adapt, and come up with new ways to use it.

In today's complex and linked world, technological power is wielded by nations as well as people and organizations. Technological power has become a major factor in a country's economic, military, and political power, since those with the best technology often have a big edge over others.

Power from technology is now an important part of everyday life. It has changed the way we talk to each other, do business, get knowledge, and even have fun. Technology has become so important to us because it makes many parts of our lives easier, faster, and more productive.

When it comes to business, technological power is very important. Companies that use cutting-edge technology can better respond to changes in the market, come up with new ideas, and stay ahead of the competition. It helps companies run more efficiently, collect and analyze data, and connect with customers better, all of which improve their chances of making money and growing.

Technology has also changed the way we talk to each other and bond with each other. Videoconferencing, instant messaging, and social media sites have become important parts of our daily lives. They let us stay in touch with friends, family, and coworkers who live far away. This linking has not only made it easier to talk to each other, but it has also created a worldwide community that goes beyond borders and cultures.

Technology gives us a lot of freedom to create new things and make progress. As technology keeps changing at a speed that has never been seen before, it opens up new ways to make progress and grow. New technologies, like AI, machine learning, virtual reality, and augmented reality, have the power to completely change businesses, solve hard problems, and make people's lives better.

As we learn more about how powerful technology is, it becomes clear that it is not just a tool or a way to get something done. With its power to change everything, it can shape our future and the very structure of society. The key is to understand its subtleties, accept its potential, and use it in a way that helps growth, inclusion, and the greater good.

Analytical Power

These days, being able to think analytically is a very useful skill. I've talked a lot about how important analytical power is for making decisions and fixing problems in this book. Now, in this chapter, I'll talk about the long-term benefits of building up this power.

New Ways of Looking at Things: As our analytical skills grow, we start to see things differently. We get good at evaluating information critically, analyzing data, and seeing things from different points of view. This change in the way we think helps us make smart choices, handle tricky situations, and comprehend the underlying factors that determine our reality.

Improving Creativity: It might not make sense to link analytical skills with creativity, since analytical skills are usually thought of as reasonable and rational skills. But being able to think logically can actually make us more creative. We can find new ways to solve problems and come up with new answers by breaking down big problems into smaller ones and looking for patterns and trends.

Problem-Solving Power: The analytical mind gives us the tools to face problems head-on. We're not scared off by how complicated things are anymore; we face them with courage and clarity. We can come up with good answers that get to the root of the problem by breaking it down into manageable pieces, finding its causes, and using logic.

Making things run more smoothly: When we're good at analyzing things, we can handle knowledge more quickly. It's easy to find the right facts, tell it apart from the noise, and come to the right conclusions. This ability to get to the important stuff more quickly and effectively helps us make choices, which saves us time and resources.

Getting rid of dangers: In today's world, where things change quickly, there are many risks. We are always having to make decisions about things we don't know, like our finances, our careers, or our personal relationships. When we have analytical power, we can look at risks and possible outcomes and make choices that have a better chance of working out. This can help us avoid mistakes that cost a lot of money and feel confident in scenarios where we don't know what will happen.

Analytical power is not a fixed skill that needs to be worked on all the time. That's how you think about and act in the world. We can develop a growth attitude by constantly improving our analytical skills, looking for new information, and questioning what we think we know. Our dedication to continuing to learn throughout our lives helps us grow as people and in our careers, allowing us to handle new situations and take advantage of new chances.

Achieving Personal and Professional Success: Ultimately, improving your analytical skills can help you achieve both personal and professional success. We become more valuable at work as we get better at solving problems, making choices, and figuring out how to get around in complicated situations. In our personal lives, we are also better able to make decisions that are in line with our ideals and make us happy.

To sum up, developing analytical power is a process that has many long-term benefits. It changes the way we think, makes us more creative, helps us solve problems, makes us more efficient, lowers our risks, encourages constant growth, and helps us reach personal and professional success in the end. By learning to improve and use our analytical skills, we can reach our full potential and confidently deal with the complicated world we live in today.

Adaptive Power

Adaptive Power is an idea that is becoming more and more important for getting through the complicated world we live in now. Being able to adapt and do well in different settings is very important in a world where things change quickly, there is uncertainty, and everything is connected. Knowing things or having skills that don't change isn't enough. We need to develop an attitude and set of skills that help us deal with the constantly changing world of our lives.

To fully understand what Adaptive Power is all about, you need to know what its parts are. You can think of adaptive power as the ability to deal with change, adversity and uncertainty and still do well. It includes a wide range of skills, traits, and attitudes that help people get along in a world that is always changing and moving quickly. It means being able to learn from mistakes, take charge, and come up with creative ways to deal with problems.

Adaptability is no longer just a nice trait to have in today's fast-paced and connected world; it's a must for success. People with Adaptive Power are better able to deal with the unexpected, take advantage of chances, and get around in today's complicated world. Being able to adapt helps people stay ahead of the curve, take advantage of new opportunities, and get past problems.

The following are some of the different parts of adaptive power:

Adaptive Power depends on having a flexible mind. It means keeping an open mind, being able to change the way we think, and being ready to look at things from different points of view and find different answers. We can better handle the complicated parts of our lives, get past cognitive limitations, and come up with new ways to solve problems if we allow our minds to be flexible.

Having emotional strength is a key part of developing Adaptive Power. It means being able to get back on your feet after a loss, deal with stress, and adjust to new situations. People can better control their emotions, keep a positive attitude, and deal with the challenges and uncertainties of life by building emotional resilience.

Adaptive Power depends on people always learning new things. In a world that is always changing, it is very important to be able to learn, unlearn, and relearn. People can stay useful, learn how to use new tools and methods, and keep improving their skills and knowledge by adopting a mindset of continuous learning.

Another important part of Adaptive Power is being resourceful. It means being able to think of creative ideas, make good use of resources, and adjust to limited resources. People can deal with problems, make the best of their situations, and come up with new ways to reach their goals by developing their creativity.

Focus on the following to build Adaptive Power:

Accepting change is a key part of building Adaptive Power. It takes developing a way of thinking and feeling that sees change as a chance to grow instead of a threat. People can deal with uncertain situations, discover new opportunities, and come up with creative answers by being open to change.

A key part of building Adaptive Power is becoming emotionally strong. It means getting better at dealing with setbacks, getting back on our feet after failing, and keeping an upbeat attitude. Building resilience helps people deal with problems, get back on track after failures, and keep going on their path to success.

Being curious helps people be flexible and keep learning. People can stay curious about the world, learn new things, and gain new views by developing their curiosity. Being curious makes you want to find new things, explore, and change with the times.

Another important part of developing Adaptive Power is learning how to solve problems. It means being able to look at complicated situations, think critically, and come up with workable answers. By getting better at solving problems, people can face obstacles with confidence and find their way through uncertain situations.

There are a number of problems that come up when adjustable power is used. Some of these problems are:

Being afraid of change can make it harder to adapt. We can stop being resistant to change and start being flexible by understanding and confronting our fears.

Having a fixed mindset can make it hard to change. Changing our focus to growth can help us develop the freedom we need for Adaptive Power.

To build Adaptive Power, you need to be aware of yourself. We can work on becoming more adaptable by being aware of our skills, weaknesses, and biases.

Being unwilling to learn can stop us from growing and changing. We can get over our resistance to learning and seize growth chances if we have a mindset of continuous development.

Because of how quickly things change in modern life, Adaptive Power is no longer just a good trait; it's a must. This book has talked about the idea of Adaptive Power, what makes it up, and how to build and use it in different areas of life. Adaptive Power is a key skill that helps people and communities do well in times of change and uncertainty. It can help with personal growth, career success, navigating uncertain situations, and making the whole group more adaptable. I really want you to think about your own Adaptive Power and enjoy the process of getting better at this important skill. There are huge benefits, like being able to handle the complicated modern world with confidence, resilience, and success.

Innovative Power

Traditionally, power meant being in charge and having authority. Today, power includes many different traits and skills that help people and groups do well when things go wrong or are unsure. Innovative power is one of these types of power. It means being able to think outside the box, solve problems, and question the status quo.

Being innovative doesn't just mean coming up with new ideas or inventions. It is a force with many aspects, including the ability to be creative, solve problems, and bring about good change. Being curious, being open to uncertainty, and not being afraid to question current rules and norms are all things that can spark innovative power. It's what drives discoveries, ideas, and adaptations that change the world.

In a world that changes so quickly, innovative power is not a nice-to-have; it's a must. As old systems fall apart and new problems appear, the ability to come up with new solutions becomes very important. People and groups with innovative power can deal with uncertainty, take advantage of opportunities, and stay ahead of the curve. It gives us the tools to solve difficult problems in creative ways and makes us stronger when things go wrong.

Innovative power is not a natural trait that only a few people have. If you have the right mindset, tools, and methods, you can build and improve this skill.

There is no straight line to innovation. There are ups and downs and twists and turns in it. The ability to fail and the ability to come up with new ideas are connected, and accepting loss can lead to growth and change. By viewing failure as an opportunity for learning and improvement, you will be driven to adopt a growth mentality, which will fuel the innovative power.

Empowerment Power

Our lives, both at home and at work, can be completely changed by empowerment power. First, we'll talk about what empowerment power means. To put it simply, empowerment means taking charge of your life, your decisions, and your actions. Realizing and using your natural strengths, skills, and potential to make the world a better place and yourself a better person is what it means. When you have empowerment power, you take charge of your life and reach true self-actualization.

Empowerment power is important in both personal and business settings. For people, empowerment power helps them get over self-doubt, set goals that they can reach, and adopt a positive attitude. It helps them become more emotionally intelligent, set and stick to limits, and talk to others better. People can reach their full potential and keep good relationships going by becoming more resilient, learning how to be a leader, and taking personal responsibility.

When it comes to work, empowerment power gives people the freedom to make decisions about their jobs and professional growth. It helps them accept differences and be open to everyone, make intelligent decisions, and develop a growth attitude. People can have a great and fulfilling career if they build a network of people who can help them, keep learning and growing, and celebrate their successes.

Empowerment power has a lot of promise, but it can also run into problems. Fear of failing and unwillingness to change are two common things that get in the way of building and using empowerment power.

Being empowered is more than just a set of skills or techniques. It's a way of thinking that affects every part of your life. Finding ways to develop an empowering power attitude is what this chapter is all about. By being open to doubt, uncertainty, and creative possibilities, people start a journey that changes them and makes them believe in their own power to empower themselves.

In the end, empowerment power is something that can change our personal and business lives in big ways. People can break through hurdles, break free from limitations, and achieve unimaginable success by tapping into this power. People can reach their full potential and make good changes in themselves and the world around them by thinking about themselves, working with others, and being open to failure. As you move toward a truly powerful life, empowerment power will help you make big changes.

Collaboration Power

Collaboration Power is the key to achieving success and influence by working together. Collaboration Power is based on working together to reach common goals. It is different from other types of power that may use force or control. Utilizing Collaboration Power has the potential to enhance many areas of daily life, ranging from improving personal relationships to making workplaces more productive and encouraging meaningful community projects.

Collaboration Power is basically being able to get along with others and work together to achieve a goal. It means working together as a team and talking to each other openly so that everyone can reach their goals. Collaboration Power is important in many areas of life because it lets people use the combined knowledge, skills, and points of view of a group. This can lead to new ideas and a sense of unity and belonging.

Collaboration Power can help you reach your personal and professional goals. In group projects, for example, different points of view and working together to solve problems can lead to new ideas. Team-building activities help people work together better and make the workplace more helpful and motivating. Collaboration Power can bring about meaningful change and use the full potential of a group when it is used in community projects. Individuals can grow as people, be successful, and feel better about their general health by working together.

Power to work together does not come without problems. Power differences, arguments, and conflicts can make it harder to work together. However, people can get past these problems and keep working together effectively by having an attitude of compromise, flexibility, and adaptability. Collaboration Power works best when people find things they agree on, listen to different points of view, and create an environment of respect and acceptance.

Collaboration Power is something that good leaders know they need to do to inspire and motivate their teams. When leaders use collaboration as a style of leadership, they make a space that supports open communication, sharing of ideas, and making decisions as a group. Collaborative leaders give their teams a sense of ownership and power, which leads to more engagement, new ideas, and total success.

To sum up, Collaboration Power is a force that can change people's lives in both their both personal and professional lives. By working together, people can reach their full potential, get past problems, and have success that has never been seen before.

Resilience Power

Resilience Power is more than just having strength or endurance. It means being able to get back up after a loss, deal with change, and do well when things go wrong. Resilience Power is a skill that may be fostered and improved over time.

Before you can fully understand Resilience Power, you need to know how it is different from other types of power. Traditional types of power may come from dominance, control, or manipulation. Resilience Power, on the other hand, comes from self-awareness, adaptability, and personal growth. It's not about controlling others; it's about being in charge of your own thoughts, emotions, and actions.

Resilience Power is composed of different components that work together to create a complete picture of strength and resilience. These parts are physical resilience, emotional resilience, and mental resilience. Each part is necessary and influences the whole, making it easier for a person to deal with problems and difficulties.

A key part of Resilience Power is building mental toughness. It includes coming up with ways to improve your attitude and way of looking at life. Thinking positively, seeing challenges as opportunities to grow, and being grateful are all good ways to strengthen your mental toughness. People who develop a resilient mindset are better able to deal with problems head-on and keep a positive mood even when things go wrong.

Another important part of Resilience Power is emotional resilience, or the ability to control and handle your feelings. To become emotionally resilient, it's important to work on your emotional intelligence, take care of yourself, and deal with stress. By knowing and controlling their emotions, people can handle tough situations better, keep relationships healthy, and deal with stress and problems in a healthy way.

It's also important to have physical resilience, which is the link between physical health and resilience power. People can improve their physical strength by taking care of their bodies by exercising regularly, eating well, and getting enough rest. A strong and healthy body is a good base for building resilience, which helps people deal with physical problems and get better after getting sick or hurt.

Reflecting on yourself is a big part of growing resilience. Self-awareness and growth can happen when people take the time to think about their feelings, thoughts, and behaviors. People can find out what their skills and weaknesses are, get rid of limiting beliefs, and gain a better understanding of themselves by doing exercises and practices that make them think about themselves. People become more aware of their own wants and resources when they think about themselves. This helps them become more resilient.

One important part of Resilience Power is adaptability. In today's world, where things are always changing, it's important to be able to accept change and deal with uncertainty. Realizing that change is a steady and unavoidable part of life can help people come up with ways to welcome it instead of fighting it. Being able to adapt to new situations, take advantage of new chances, and stay flexible when things are uncertain are all important ways to build resilience.

Being resilient isn't just an idea or a theory; it's something you can feel. Resilience Power is something that many people have shown throughout history when they were facing huge problems and difficulties. Their stories of how they overcame hardships are motivational and teach us important lessons. These people, like Nelson Mandela's unwavering determination while he was in jail and Malala Yousafzai's unwavering determination to fight for girls' education despite facing violence and persecution, are great examples of Resilience Power and remind us all of the strength and resilience that we have inside us.

A big part of building Resilience Power is getting rid of ideas that hold you back. These limiting beliefs, which are often based on fear or doubt in oneself, can make it harder to get over failures and accept change. People can break free from their limitations and reach their full potential by recognizing and questioning their limiting beliefs. Believing in yourself and your ability to get through any problem or task that comes your way is what resilience power is all about.

It is very important to help kids and teens build resilience power. Parents, teachers, and mentors can give kids the tools and attitude they need to deal with life's challenges by teaching them to be resilient from a young age. Teaching kids to accept failure, get over setbacks, and have a growth mindset gives them the strength to deal with problems head-on and builds a strong basis for being resilient for the rest of their lives. We can make sure the future is better and more stable by teaching the next generation to be strong.

To sum up, Resilience Power is a force that can change people's lives in both emotional and professional ways. It means being able to get back up after a loss, deal with change, and do well when things go wrong. People can reach their full potential, get past obstacles, and have unimaginable success by building their resilience power. Individuals can create a future where resilience is the basis for building a better and more connected world by accepting that resilience power can help people grow as individuals and as a group. Let's accept Resilience Power and use it to improve ourselves and each other in our daily lives.

Influence Power

Influence power is the ability to sway, inspire, and shape other people's views, behaviors, and decisions. Influence power is not something that only a few people have; anyone who wants to make a lasting impact on the world can learn and master it.

Influence power is a broad idea that includes many different types and sources. It shows up in various ways, depending on the person, the scenario, or even the way they think. For example, social influence comes from the way our relationships work and the power systems that protect them. The study of psychological influence, on the other hand, looks into how the mind works and how it reacts to being manipulated and persuaded. Furthermore, situational influence explores how external circumstances and contexts can shape and change the dynamics of power.

When you want to affect someone, you need to build trust and credibility. Without them, everything we do to persuade others will fall apart like a house of cards. Being real, honest, and consistent are all things that help build and maintain trust. We can get closer to others and earn their trust and love by making real connections with them and being honest with them all the time. No one should take the time to build trust and credibility because it takes a careful mix of empathy, honesty, and self-awareness.

Talking to people is what gives influence power its life. We can use the art of good communication to weave a web of words that capture people's hearts and thoughts. People with a lot of influence need to be able to show empathy, listen actively, and be clear. Understanding the nuances of verbal and nonverbal communication, as well as tailoring our message to the needs and wants of our audience, can raise our persuasive prowess to unprecedented heights.

People have been telling stories for a very long time. Stories have the power to connect people across borders and capture their hearts and thoughts. We can create stories that really connect with our audience, making them feel things, making them think, and moving them to take action by using the power of storytelling. When told well, a story can go beyond facts and paint a detailed picture that speaks to our deepest selves. We can put other people in a world of possibilities through stories, which can spark their imagination and make them want to align their views and actions with ours.

There will always be opposition and problems on the way to gain influence power. They put our resolve to the test, poke at our weak spots, and make us question ourselves. To get through these problems, we need to be strong, determined, and able to change how we do things. We can break down barriers and make progress toward our goals by coming up with plans and strategies to deal with objections and pushback head-on. In the face of trouble, our unwavering determination is what gives us influence power that goes beyond boundaries.

Influence power is not a temporary thing; it's something that you strive for your whole life. We need to be flexible, strong, and aware of how things are changing around us if we want to keep our influence. We can make sure that our power to influence lasts by being open to change, adapting our methods, and staying in touch with the wants and needs of the people we want to change. Being able to adapt and think ahead are important for getting through the changing currents of influence and coming out stronger than ever.

Diplomatic Power

Diplomatic power is the skill of dealing with other people politely, with empathy, and with integrity, which builds trust and credibility. People must be careful when they dance the complicated dance of diplomacy, because every step can either build bridges or burn them down.

To fully understand the complexities of diplomatic power, it is necessary to look into what it means and how it works. There are many parts and aspects of diplomatic power that work together to make a force of influence. Some of these skills are good communication, handling conflicts, negotiating, and the ability to make partnerships and networks. All of these things make diplomatic power stronger and more useful overall, letting people control the steps of exchanges and get the results they want.

There are some unique problems that come up when people from different cultures connect with each other. To have good cross-cultural interactions, you need to understand and respect cultural differences. Diplomatic power helps people understand and respect each other's cultures, accept differences, and work toward understanding and respect.

To sum up, diplomatic power is a complex force that shapes relationships, affects results, and promotes good change. It's an art that needs empathy, the ability to communicate clearly, the ability to handle conflicts, and the skill to make connections and partnerships. Diplomatic power isn't just used between two people; it's also used in business, in personal relationships, and even in world politics. People can build trust and credibility and make a real difference in the world by learning the factors of diplomatic power.

Artistic Power

Beyond the everyday, artistic power takes us to a magical world where imagination, creation, and expression are the most important things. Some people are driven by this force when they are brave enough to go deep into their souls and follow the call of their artistic destiny. Artistic power isn't just for artists and creative people; anyone who wants to tap into their deepest creative potential can use it.

At the heart of artistic power are three important parts that work together to make a symphony of stunning creativity. These things—creativity, imagination, and expression—are what make art powerful and help it to grow and show itself in its truest form.

Being creative is what gives art its power. It's what starts the fire of inspiration and drives us to come up with new thoughts, ideas, and dreams. Being creative frees us from the rules of society so we can go our own way. It pushes us to think outside the box, question how things have always been done, and make new and interesting things.

Imagination is where artistic power grows. The valuable gem lets us travel through the unseen worlds, picture vivid scenes and people, and bring abstract ideas to life. Without the limits of reality, our imaginations are like a playground full of endless possibilities. They let us experience the vastness of our dreams and desires.

It is through expression that the power of art can be heard. Communication is the way we share our feelings, thoughts, and ideas with the world. Expression can come in many forms, such as brush strokes on a painting, words woven into poems, or melodies made by a musician. It's what gets our message across, touching people deeply, making them feel things, and making a connection with the bigger picture of life.

Deep down in everyone's soul is a source of creative energy that, when tapped into and developed, can unleash amazing artistic power. It is a power that comes from outside of our personal and work lives and adds a magical touch to everything we do.

When you accept your artistic power, you open the door to a journey of self-discovery, self-expression, and personal growth. You have to be brave to explore the uncharted areas of your own creativity, to enjoy the infinite depths of your imagination, and to share your unique artistic voice with the world without shame.

Before you step on the edge of your artistic power, remember that it has the power to change not only your life but also the lives of those who see your work. It is a force that can light a spark in other people, encouraging them to explore their own creative potential and start their own artistic travels.

So, I invite you to feel the power of your art and let it lead you to a world full of endless options. Let your imagination, originality, and expression all come together to make a path of artistic brilliance that is all your own. Accept the beauty of your unique artistic style and let it connect with others and make them feel amazed.

You already have the power; you just need to wake it up. Accept it, take care of it, and let it shine creatively, magically, and transformatively into your world.

Creative Power

The key to unlocking unimaginable potential and turning the ordinary into the extraordinary lies within each of us: creative power. There is a force that goes beyond typical power structures because it doesn't reside in physical strength or dominance, but in creativity, inspiration, and innovation. Creative power sparks changes and keeps people going on their never-ending journey of self-discovery and exploration.

Before we can fully understand how powerful creative power is, we need to first define what it is. At its core, creative power is the ability to come up with new and life-changing ideas and share them with the world. In addition to art, it affects all areas of human life.

Thinking outside the box, questioning norms, and making new paths are all made possible by our creativity, which is the heart of creative power. It is the spark that sets our imaginations on fire and takes us beyond the limits of what we know into the world of endless potential. When we use our creativity, it makes us bring unique additions to the world.

To fully use our creative power, we need to know where it comes from and what makes it go. The first part of creative power is inspiration, which leads us to new ideas and points of view. That which pulls at our hearts is the divine whisper, which makes us curious and starts the fire of creation.

As the second pillar, imagination is the rich dirt where creative power can grow and take root. Our thoughts are like an endless playground, full of fantastical worlds and endless possibilities. Imagination leads to new ideas and lets us imagine and make the impossible.

The third pillar is intuition. It's like an internal compass that points us toward truths that seem unseen and go beyond reasoning and reason. This is the voice that comes from deep inside and guides us toward the ways that are in line with our true selves and deepest desires.

Through the world of creative power, there are always things that get in the way. Even the smartest people can get stuck when they hit creative blocks, which are things that get in the way of their ideas and motivation. To get past these problems is to use our creative power to its fullest.

Identifying common challenges and limits to creative potential is the first step toward overcoming them. Recognizing these blockages, whether they are self-doubt, perfectionism, or fear of judgment, allows us to actively work toward their removal.

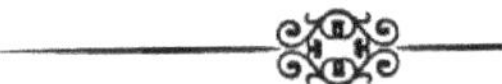

Strategic Power

Strategic power is a concept that is extremely important in our daily lives, but we may not be aware of it. It's the skill of knowing, analyzing, and using different kinds of power to get what we want out of life and get through the complicated situations we face. You don't have to be in a place of authority or be an expert in a certain field to have strategic power. Anyone who is willing to learn more about it can develop it.

Finding the power sources in a situation, knowing how power relationships affect results, and being able to use these relationships to our benefit are all parts of strategic power. It means understanding the pros and cons of each party and planning how to use that knowledge to change the course of events.

To improve our strategic power, we need to develop a strategic attitude. It needs us to look at things in a big picture and ahead, always looking for ways to grow and improve things. A strategic mindset helps us find hidden trends and see problems coming, which lets us make smart choices.

To get the most out of our strategic power, we must first figure out what our strategic goals are. Strategic goals are those that fit with our bigger picture and take into account all the things that affect our path. They are clear, measured, attainable, important, and have a due date. Setting strategic goals helps us decide what to work on first and how to best use our resources.

Power dynamics are a big part of how things turn out in many cases. When we understand these processes, we can handle complicated situations and use our power wisely. By looking at how power is distributed and how it affects each other, we can find opportunities, predict problems, and come up with plans that will help us reach our goals.

To keep strategic power, it's important to think about and get ready for problems. By getting ready for possible problems, we can lessen their effects and put ourselves in a better position to solve them. To do this, we need to do thorough risk assessments, make backup plans, and keep looking at our strategies.

Information is a useful way to improve strategic power. We have an advantage over our competitors because we can gather, analyze, and make sense of important information. We can make educated decisions and come up with strategies that work with changing conditions if we keep up with industry trends, market dynamics, and new technologies.

In conclusion, strategic power is a complicated notion with enormous potential in our lives. We can use its power to reach our goals, make a difference, and get through the challenges of life with confidence and purpose if we understand how it works and develop the skills and attitude that are needed. Strategic power gives us the ability to control our own lives and make a future that fits with our greatest hopes.

Visionary Power

Visionary power is the ability to see beyond the present moment and envisage a daring, inspirational, and transformational future. Visionary Power gives us the power to create our own future and open the door to a world of endless opportunities.

Visionary Power holders can think big, not be limited by normal ways of thinking, and have the courage to dream on a huge scale. Their dreams are not just wild guesses; they are detailed plans for a better future that get people excited and inspired to take action. Visionary leaders give those who follow them a sense of purpose and direction through the way they speak and write.

Before we can get Visionary Power, we need to develop a growth attitude. Believing that our potential is unlimited and that we can always grow and learn is something we need to do. We can think more creatively and open to new ideas when we look for new situations and different points of view. Meditation, visualizing, and journaling are some other things that can help us connect with our inner visionary.

Visionary Power is really powerful when it can motivate and inspire other people. Visionary leaders have a magnetic pull on people around them, effortlessly instilling a spark of enthusiasm and motivation in their teams. They are gifted at communicating clearly and convincingly, telling others about their vision and encouraging them to take action to help them reach their common goals.

But there are some things that can go wrong when you try to build and use Visionary Power. Self-doubt and opposition from others can make it hard to see the big picture. But true thinkers are strong enough to get past these problems and stay true to their vision even when things go wrong or people don't believe in it. They keep going because they are strong and believe in their purpose, which helps them lead their teams to success.

Developing a visionary attitude is important for getting the most out of Visionary Power. Visionary thinking is based on three things: curiosity, imagination, and an open mind. We can be more visionary if we look for different points of view, see failure as a chance to learn, and encourage a culture of innovation. This will help us think outside the box of custom and change the world around us.

Visionary Power is a force that lives inside of us and is just ready to be awakened. Through developing and using this power, we can make a world that is even better than we could have imagined. With Visionary Power, we can leave a long mark on the world and have a big effect on it. Let's accept our visionary potential and start a journey of growth, change, and endless possibilities.

Motivational Power

Within each of us is a force called motivational power that is just waiting to be unleashed. It's what lights the fire in our heart and drives us to achieve success and happiness in our lives. Motivational Power is different from other types of power because it is not given to us by outside forces. Instead, it is grown inside of us.

The thing that pushes us to act, go the extra mile, and keep going even when things get hard is our motivational power. It's the fire inside us that makes us want to dream big and do great things. The thing that drives us to succeed is our motivational power.

You can't say enough about how important motivation is for success. Without motivation, our dreams stay dormant and we don't use all of our potential. Our efforts are fueled by motivation, which helps us get past problems and limitations. We stay focused, strong, and determined to reach our goals because of this force. Without motivation, success is just a vague idea that you can never quite reach.

Motivation is different from other kinds of power because it comes from within us and can be controlled and grown. It doesn't depend on outside forces or other people's permission. Motivational power comes from our personal beliefs, wants, and goals, while other types of power may come from authority, influence, or control over resources. This power is personal and specific to each person. Anyone can use it if they would like to.

The Psychology of Motivation looks at the ideas and theories that help us understand what motivates people. Some of these theories, like Maslow's hierarchy of needs and Herzberg's two-factor theory, help us understand what motivates us and why we do the things we do. By looking into these ideas, we can learn more about what drives us and what drives other people, which helps us in both our personal and professional lives. You can learn more about the idea of Motivational Power in the book The Ultimate Book of Motivation.

Motivating yourself has a lot of effects on your health and happiness. Following our interests and finding meaning in life keeps us motivated and makes sure that our work is in line with what makes us happy and fulfilled. To stay motivated, balancing personal and professional goals keeps us from getting burned out and makes sure that we give all parts of our lives the care they need. Using motivation to take care of our physical, mental, and emotional health makes sure that our motivations last, which lets us thrive and attain real happiness.

You will learn new things, grow, and change as you go through Motivational Power. We are in charge of our own success and happiness when we use the power that lies within us. Motivation pushes us forward and helps us get past problems, reach great heights, and leave a lasting impression. It is up to us to use our Motivational Power, accept our visionary potential, and start a path of growth, change, and endless possibilities.

Radiant Power

Radiant Power is a concept that goes beyond physical strength and influence. It's a force that comes from inside you, like a glow that draws people to you. People respect and want to do something when they see them. However, what is Radiant Power exactly, and how can it be used to its fullest?

Radiant Power isn't just about having a strong personality or being physically imposing; it's also about having an inner light that shows us the way and draws people to us.

A key part of using Radiant Power is having confidence. It means having faith in your own skills and knowing that you can handle any problem that comes your way. Being confident gives us the courage to try new things, take risks, and follow our dreams with unwavering determination. We can't help but notice how confident it makes us feel, and its powerful presence makes it impossible to ignore.

Radiant Power is shown through presence. People are drawn to people who are fully engaged and present in the present moment and who exude a sense of purpose and confidence. Being present helps us connect deeply with others, listen attentively, and communicate effectively. This way of being gives off strength and influence, drawing people to us and leaving an image that lasts.

Radiant Power isn't just for one-on-one conversations; it also affects how we relate to other people. It's the skill of making good bonds with other people, to motivate and encourage those around us. By showing Radiant Power in our relationships and interactions, we spread happiness and empowerment, changing the lives of those we meet for the better.

Problem-solving Power

When I learned more about power, I came across a concept that really interested me: problem-solving power. People usually think of authority, influence, or physical strength when they think of power. But the ability to deal with life's problems and find answers is just as powerful. Problem-solving power gives people the ability to get past problems, make intelligent decisions, and make the world a better place.

Problem-solving power is basically being able to recognize, understand, and successfully solve different problems and issues. It includes being able to think critically, be creative, be resourceful, and be able to change. By using their problem-solving skills, people can easily get through tough situations and get past problems.

Problem-solving isn't just a bunch of random steps put together; it's a planned process that needs careful attention and strategic thought.

Before trying to find answers, it's important to fully understand what the problem is and how complicated it is. By doing a complete evaluation, people can find the problem's root causes, weigh the risks that might come up, and figure out what factors are at play.

One important part of being able to solve problems is being able to think outside the box and come up with more than one answer.

Now that you have a list of possible options, the next important step is to evaluate them and pick the best one. By thinking about each option carefully, people can be sure to pick the one that will lead to the best result.

Finding the best solution is only the first step; implementing it correctly is what makes the problem-solving process work. A well-executed implementation plan is essential for getting things done. It helps with everything from making action plans and assigning jobs to dealing with problems and tracking progress.

Problem-solving doesn't end when an answer is put into action; it requires a constant effort to look back at what happened and learn from it. People can improve their ability to solve problems over time by having a growth mindset and constantly seeking feedback.

As I finish this part of my book, I think about how powerful it is to be able to solve problems. It's a power that knows no limits and gives people the strength to face challenges, make changes, and get through hard times. We can reach our full potential and start a journey of growth, collaboration, and personal satisfaction when we use our problem-solving skills. With creative thought, analytical skills, and a growth mindset, we can get through life's challenges and come out on the other side as strong problem-solvers and positive change agents.

Transformational Power

Transformational power, at its core, is what makes things change. We move from a state of stagnation to one of growth and change because of this force. It makes us want to question conventional norms, fight limiting beliefs, and go exploring in new and unknown areas. When we are given transformational power, we become aware of our untapped potential and are inspired to live a life with meaning, authenticity, and satisfaction.

One of the most important things about transformational power is that it can encourage and drive change. It gives us a strong desire to change and grow, which pushes us toward a better version of ourselves. It gives us the strength to leave our comfort zones, face our fears, and welcome the unknown because of its changing energy. Transformational power gives us a new sense of purpose and makes us want to follow our dreams and goals without stopping.

There are many different places where transformational power can come from. Beliefs, values, and events that are unique to each person store transformational power that helps us grow and learn about ourselves. What we believe affects how we see ourselves and the world around us. When we use our beliefs to get what we want, they can change things in a powerful way. Our beliefs give us direction for what to do and how to make choices. They also help us grow as people. Furthermore, all of our events, good and bad, teach us important lessons that help us change.

When we come to it, creative power is something that can change and improve every part of our lives. It helps us get past our limits, see our real potential, and live a life with meaning, growth, and satisfaction. When we connect with the deep source of transformative power that lives inside us, we become change agents who encourage others to start their own transformative paths. When we learn to control and use this power, we not only grow as people, but we also help make the world a better place for everyone.

Change Power

Change Power is the ability to make changes that matter and last in many areas of our lives, such as our relationships, workplaces, communities, and even within ourselves.

To understand Change Power, you must first define what it means. Change power means being able to start, drive, and keep change going. It's about having the guts to question the way things are, the ideas and systems that are in place, and to imagine a different future. It means facing the discomfort of not knowing what will happen and accepting the unknown in order to grow and move forward. Change Power takes a strong sense of purpose, a strong belief in one's own ability to make things better, and a strong will to get past problems and push the limits.

Getting Change Power is not something you can do by yourself; it's a process that needs you to keep learning, growing, and contemplating. It requires us to know our own skills, weaknesses, and areas where we can improve. To do that, you have to be willing to be vulnerable and let go of limiting ideas and self-imposed limits. Getting Change Power means learning useful skills like how to communicate, persuade, negotiate, and solve conflicts. These skills can give us the power to move through and change the world around us.

Once we have Change Power, we need to figure out how to use it well. To do this, we need to know how to use this power to make good changes in our lives and the world around us that last. Using Change Power takes a plan, a clear vision, and the ability to get other people excited about and involved in our cause. It asks us to learn how to balance drive with compassion, kindness with boldness, and rigidity with adaptability.

We can not only make good changes by using Change Power well, but we can also motivate and inspire others to do the same.

When you have Change Power, you have to get past people's unwillingness to change. Some people may be against us questioning the accepted rules, beliefs, and systems because they are afraid of the unknown or want to keep things the same. To get past this resistance, we need to be patient, persistent, and able to explain our goal and get other people to join us. To do this, you need to build strong relationships, encourage trust, and address the fears and worries of people who might be against change. We can find common ground and make a change-friendly setting by responding to resistance with understanding and empathy.

To sum up, Change Power is a force that has the power to change and improve every part of our lives. When we learn to control and use this power, we not only grow as people, but we also help make the world a better place for everyone. To change power, we have to use our inner resources, face our fears and limits, and be open to being hurt. As we develop our own transformative power, we become change agents who encourage others to accept their own transformative potential. Harnessing and using Change Power as a group not only makes positive changes in our immediate surroundings, but it also helps the bigger movements toward a more fair and sustainable world.

Ethical Power

At its core, ethical power is the ability to affect and influence other people in a way that is morally right and in line with a set of ethical standards. It is a power that goes beyond making money for yourself and focuses on making friends and building trust with others. Being honest, having integrity, being open, and caring about the well-being of everyone concerned are all parts of ethical power.

Ethical power is a very important part of personal as well as professional relationships for keeping things healthy and productive. It helps people accept, respect, and understand each other. Without moral strength, relationships can fall apart because of lies, trickery, and self-interest.

To gain and use ethical power in our daily lives, we need to have a deep knowledge of moral principles, good communication skills, emotional intelligence, and a strong desire to keep learning and growing. Power that can't be gained quickly but must be built up over time through conscious effort and a firm commitment to moral behavior.

The idea of ethical power comes from a set of rules that help people make decisions and act in a good way. Being honest, having ethics, and being open are the building blocks of ethical power. Being sincere and telling the truth in our interactions is what it means to be honest. Being honest means having integrity, which means that our actions should match our ideals. Being open and responsible in how we deal with others is what transparency means.

These moral values are more than just words; they shape who we are and how we act. They are a steady reminder of how important it is to be kind, respectful, and understanding to others. By following these rules, we not only gain moral strength but also make the world a better place.

Trust is the link between people who have moral power and the rest of us. It's not possible for ethical power to work without trust. To build trust, you need to be consistent, dependable, and genuinely care about other people's well-being. It means taking responsibility for our deeds and being clear about what we want to do.

Credibility, on the other hand, comes from being knowledgeable, skilled, and having a history of doing the right thing. For trust to grow, this is what it takes. People are more likely to believe in and value our ethical power when we show that we are smart and ethical.

Growth Power

Growth Power is different from the other types of power this book talks about because it focuses on personal and professional growth. It includes the path of always getting better and the search for growth in all areas of life. It is not about controlling or dominating other people. Instead, it is about using your strengths to be successful and happy.

To develop your Growth Power, you need to have a growth mindset. It means encouraging people to believe that they can improve their skills and knowledge through commitment, hard work, and persistence. People who have a growth mindset are open to new challenges, see failures as chances to learn and grow, and keep their attention on learning and getting better.

Fears and ideas that hold us back can stop us from growing as people and keep us from using our Growth Power. It is important to recognize these problems and work to solve them, knowing that our potential is not limited by the limits we set for ourselves. We can reach our full potential if we believe ideas that make us feel good and come up with ways to deal with our fears.

Mentors and role models are very important for our personal growth and for getting Growth Power. Asking people who have already done what we want to do for advice can give us useful information, support, and motivation. We grow and develop faster when we have important mentorship relationships and learn from other people's experiences.

Growth Power is a way of life, not something you get one time. To really use Growth Power, we need to make it a part of our everyday lives. This means using our personal growth and development to improve our relationships, overall health, and professional achievements. When we consciously use the new ideas and skills we've gained through personal growth, we make a positive difference in the lives of many others.

To sum up, Growth Power is a force that can change things and help people grow personally and professionally. You need to have a growth mindset, set meaningful goals, form good habits, keep learning, be resilient, and be able to inspire others. We can reach our full potential, be happy, and make a difference in the world if we commit to personal improvement. Growth Power isn't just a place you get to; it's a trip you take to learn more about yourself, make progress, and change.

Reputational Power

There is a secret gem in the vast world of power dynamics: a force that goes beyond money, power, and physical strength. What kind of power comes from whispers of respect and admiration? That kind of power is called reputational power.

For those who want to gain power and influence, a good image based on honesty, dependability, and moral behavior is an essential asset. It's the thing that gets things done, makes deals possible, and opens doors to success. A good reputation draws chances your way, helps you make connections, and earns the respect of others. It gives other people confidence, which makes them more likely to join forces with a trustworthy person. On the other hand, a bad reputation can hurt confidence, break up relationships, and slow down progress, leaving people stuck on a lonely path to insignificance.

Not everyone can build a strong and trustworthy image overnight. It needs to be done carefully, with steadfast dedication and care in all actions and choices. Brick by brick, a reputation is built by cultivating basic principles, acting consistently and honorably, and demonstrating competence and talents. Being honest with others is important because it lets your real character shine through and leaves an indelible mark on those you meet. Making an image that lasts by always being honest, giving great value, and keeping their promises are all things that people can do.

Even if someone has a strong reputation, it can still get hurt by bad decisions or bad luck. People may be dealing with a damaged image and desperately looking for ways to make things right. To fix a bad image, you have to put in a lot of work, be humble, and really want to make things right. It requires showing that you have changed your behavior, being honest, and being willing to listen to the worries of those who are affected. People can build the grit they need to get over their mistakes and earn back the trust of others by being persistent, patient, and dedicated to growth.

Maintaining a strong and powerful reputation is not something you can only do for a short time. It takes constant work, a desire to improve yourself, and awareness of the fine line between self-interest and the greater good. People must constantly work to improve their image while being aware of the possible outcomes of their actions. People can strengthen their image and make sure it lasts for a long time by staying true to their core values, being flexible when things change, and always being trustworthy.

Being strong in reputational power means having power that comes from being honest and doing the right thing. People should not underestimate the power of their reputation, because it has the ability to either make their life very important or not important at all. By learning about this power, developing it, and using it in an honest way, you can unlock its endless potential and find your way to real influence and lasting effects.

Adaptive Power

The ability to deal with the challenges of daily life is known as adaptive power. It is a key skill for success and happiness. Unlike the other types of power this book talks about, like positional or persuasive power, adaptive power is not about controlling other people. Instead, it's about being able to change and do well in any situation by being resilient, flexible, and good at solving problems. People can improve their overall effectiveness in many areas of their lives by building adaptive power. This will help them deal with change, get past problems, and make better decisions.

There are several important parts of adaptive power that work together to make a strong foundation for personal growth and success. Some of these are adaptability, resilience, and the ability to solve problems. People who are flexible can adjust to new situations, and people who are resilient can get back up after problems or failures. Problem-solving skills let you come up with creative answers and get past problems. By making each of these parts stronger, people can build a strong base for flexible power that will help them handle the challenges of life with ease.

Uncertainty and change are natural parts of life. Developing adaptive power helps people handle these problems with grace and strength. People can grow and change by being open to uncertainty and change. They can use these lessons to change themselves and their careers. Some things that can really help you adapt and do well even when things are unclear are keeping an open mind, keeping a positive attitude, and asking for help.

Adaptive power can help and empower others, which can have a good effect on both personal and professional relationships. People can motivate and inspire those around them by using adaptable power to create a culture of flexibility and strength. People can give others the tools they need to accept change, deal with problems, and develop their own adaptive power by teaching, coaching, and setting a good example.

To sum up, adaptive power is a force that changes people and helps them handle the challenges of life with grace, agility, and endurance. People can improve their personal and professional growth, make better decisions, and build strong relationships by working on the key parts of adaptability, such as being flexible, resilient, and good at fixing problems. People can unlock the unlimited potential of adaptive power and find their way to real influence and lasting effect if they are committed to always learning, have a growth mindset, and act in an ethical way.

Psychological Power

Though it doesn't exist in the physical world, psychological power is a force that goes deep into people's minds. It's not power through force or coercion, but through knowing and controlling the psychological processes that make people act the way they do. It's a power that can change how people think, feel, and believe, which can then affect what other people think and do.

Influence is one of the most important ideas in psychological power. Influence means being able to persuade, convince, and lead other people to do what you want them to do. It means knowing what other people want, what scares them, and what drives them, and then using that information to connect and speak with them in a good way. You can motivate people, bring about change, and reach goals that you might not have thought were possible without impact.

However, getting psychological power is not easy and comes with a lot of difficulties. To do it, you need to know a lot about human psychology and be able to find your way through the complicated webs of feelings, beliefs, and perceptions. With this knowledge, you can send messages, make up stories, and use small cues to change how other people see and react to you.

A big part of psychological power is how people think and believe. Their effect on our ideas, feelings, and actions shapes how we see the world. You can change how other people see you and the world around you by taking control of these perception filters. One way to do this is to carefully change the information, frame it, and use persuasion tactics.

The path to using psychological power, on the other hand, is not free of problems and difficulties. The potential for manipulation, loss of authenticity, and retribution are all crucial factors to consider while using psychological power responsibly. To stay honest and moral, and to make sure that your actions and behaviors are always in line with your beliefs and goals, it is very important. By staying alert, self-aware, and mindful, people can deal with the complicated world of psychological power while reducing the bad effects that might happen.

The result is that psychological power is a complex force that exists in the mind and affects how people think, feel, and act. It means being able to persuade, influence, and lead other people to the result you want. But using psychological power in a good way takes a deep understanding of how people think and feel, as well as an awareness of right and wrong and a desire to keep growing and getting better. People can improve their personal and professional growth, make important connections, and make the world a better place by developing their psychological power.

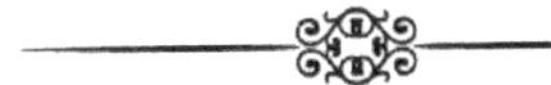

Time Management Power

When people are good at managing their time, they can get morc done, feel less stressed, and reach their goals. This is called time management power. Making intelligent choices about how to spend your time is possible if you know how to do this. Not like other resources, time is limited and can't be saved or won back. To make the most of your time for personal growth and success, you need to know what it's really worth.

Before you can master time management, you need to figure out what activities and habits waste your time and get rid of them. Things like using social media too much, putting things off, and not being organized can make you less efficient and less productive. Time-wasters not only waste useful time, but they also waste useful mental energy on things that aren't useful. People can better manage their time and focus on things that really matter if they can find and get rid of these time-wasters.

Another important part of mastering time management power is making a method for keeping track of time. Setting clear goals, putting jobs in order of importance, and making a schedule or to-do list are all parts of this. Setting limits and staying away from too much responsibility also helps people stay focused and avoid burnout. A well-organized method for managing time gives people the tools they need to make the most of their time and make sure that important tasks get the attention they need.

One well-known way to better control your time is the Pomodoro Technique. For this method, work is split into chunks of 25 minutes, with short breaks in between. Short, focused bursts of work are usually more productive than long, unbroken times, so this method helps people stay focused. The Pomodoro Technique not only makes people more productive, but it also keeps their minds from getting tired, which lets them work faster and get better results.

Another thing that can help you manage your time well is delegating and outsourcing chores. Realizing that you can't do everything yourself and putting your trust in other people to handle certain tasks can help you make more time for activities that are more important to you. By delegating and outsourcing, people can use the knowledge and skills of others, which increases output and efficiency in the long run. For delegation and outsourcing to work, there needs to be good communication and clear standards.

Setting limits and knowing how to say "no" are important parts of being able to manage your time well. People often feel like they have too many responsibilities and duties that take up their time and energy. People can protect their time and focus on what's important by setting limits and putting jobs in order of importance. To keep a good work-life balance and avoid taking on too much, you need to learn how to say "no" to requests or activities that aren't necessary. It's not a sign of weakness to say "no." Instead, it shows that you know yourself and can set your goals and values first.

Getting rid of distractions is a key skill for improving your time management. In this modern age, there are a lot of things that can distract you and make you less productive. Setting aside a specific area to work, using productivity tools and apps, and practicing mindfulness are all good ways to stay focused and reduce distractions. Distractions can get in the way of people staying on task and making the most of their time.

Energy management is an important part of time management that is often forgotten. Taking care of your health by doing things like eating well, getting enough sleep, and doing regular physical exercise are all part of managing your energy levels. People can work at their best when they are aware of their energy levels throughout the day and plan their tasks around them. Keeping track of your energy levels is important for staying focused, avoiding burnout, and getting the most done.

Putting things off is a regular problem that makes it hard to manage your time well. It's possible to stop putting things off by figuring out what causes it and then using tactics to stop it. Setting deadlines, breaking projects down into smaller, more manageable steps, and setting up systems for accountability are all good ways to stop putting things off and keep working.

To sum up, Time Management Power is a strong force that, when used correctly, can lead to great success in your personal as well as professional life. People can improve their time management skills by realizing how important time is, finding and getting rid of activities that waste time, setting up a time management system, and using techniques like the Pomodoro Technique. Setting limits, delegating chores, and dealing with distractions are all important ways to stay focused and avoid taking on too much. Planning, organizing, and setting priorities well are all important parts of being able to handle your time well. Managing energy levels, thinking about things, and using technology all make time management even more powerful. Long-term success in time management comes from not putting things off, keeping a healthy work-life mix, and committing to always getting better. Mastering time management is a journey that is always changing, and you have to keep working on yourself and adapting. People can make the most of their time, reach their goals, and reach their full potential if they work hard to learn and improve their time management skills.

Communication Power

Communication Power is important for getting what you want, being in charge, and getting along with other people. Clear communication helps us say what we want to say, get our thoughts and ideas across, and connect with others more deeply. Because of this power, we can make a difference in our personal and professional lives that lasts.

There are many parts to Communication Power, and each one is very important to how well we communicate overall. The words we use to talk to each other have a lot of power to get our thoughts across. Others, though, often remember things about you that you don't say, like your body language, facial expressions, and tone of voice. Another important thing that helps people communicate well is actively listening with a sincere desire to understand and relate. Also, knowing the situation in which communication takes place helps us make sure that our messages are acceptable.

For conversation to work, people need to be clear and sure of themselves. When we talk to each other clearly, we say what we mean in a way that leaves no room for confusion or misunderstanding. The best way to do this is to use clear words, organize our thoughts well, and pay attention to our body language. When we're sure of how to say something, we can say it with conviction and confidence, which engages others and builds trust.

You can't say enough good things about active listening. Giving someone our full attention and really hearing what they have to say makes them feel valuable and helps us see things from their point of view. By paraphrasing and asking for clarification, we show that we care about the topic and are invested in it, which builds relationships and makes communication more effective.

A lot of the time, body language speaks stronger than words. We show how we really feel and what we want to say through our body language, facial movements, and tone of voice. Being aware of how our body language affects others and using it on purpose can make our conversation much more effective.

Communication Power is very helpful when trying to solve problems and reach agreements. Effective communication makes it possible to actively solve problems, handle conflicts with understanding and respect, and find answers that work for everyone.

At work, Communication Power helps build better professional relationships, make teams work better, and boost productivity.

Getting past barriers to conversation is a must for good communication. Problems can arise because of differences in culture, language, and misunderstandings, but these can be solved by being flexible and using good communication skills.

Using the ideas in Communication Power in our everyday lives will always lead to good results and better relationships. Effective communication helps us understand each other, opens doors, and lets us be our true selves, whether we're at work, with friends and family, or in our personal lives. Accepting Communication Power helps us get through complicated interactions with other people and reach our full potential.

Chapter Seven

The Future of Power

In this section, I go into detail about the complicated link between new technologies and the way power works. There's no doubt that technology has changed the way we live, work, and talk to each other. In a world that is always changing, it is important to understand how these new technologies affect power.

The rise of digital monitoring is one of the most important ways that technology has changed power. The ability to spy on people has become easier and more advanced thanks to progress in technology. Governments and businesses now have access to our personal information like never before. This lets them keep an eye on us, change how we act, and keep control. From the ubiquitous CCTV cameras to data mining algorithms, surveillance has been turned into a tool to show who is in charge and silence those who disagree. We are all being watched all the time these days thanks to technology. Those who control this monitoring technology have more power than ever.

Also, you should never forget how powerful information can be. The digital age has made it easier for everyone to get knowledge, which has leveled the playing field in the race for power. People and groups can get to a huge amount of information with just a few clicks, which gives them the power to challenge conventional power structures. Getting and using information in a smart way has become a powerful source of power. In this age of information, people who know how to properly analyze and make sense of data are the ones who can open up new possibilities and break down old hierarchies.

Social media sites have become a major tool for shaping public opinion and getting people to join groups. They have an incredible amount of power over the people. People can get a lot of followers on Facebook, Twitter, Instagram, and other sites, become influential, and question the way power works in the world. Social media is powerful because it can bring together people with similar views, give a voice to those who didn't have one before, and start large-scale efforts for social and political change. On the other hand, social media can be dangerous because it can be used to control our views, create "echo chambers," and cause people to disagree with each other. This delicate balance between power and effect shows how much technology changes the way we see the world.

However, it is also important to see the bad things about technology. In the world of cyber attacks, it is clear that technology can be used for bad things. Hackers with advanced technology can get into computer systems, steal private data, stop important services from working, and even bring whole countries to their knees. They have power that can't be seen or touched, but it's just as dangerous because it can hurt countries and threaten national security. The conflict between people who want to gain power through cyber warfare and people whose job it is to protect against it is always changing.

When it comes to fighting, technological progress has changed the balance of power between countries. Those who have advanced defense technology are ahead of those who don't, which strengthens their dominance and could cause changes in geopolitics. Nations with cutting-edge technology, like robotic aerial vehicles and cyberwarfare tools, can control the world and change the way politics are played around the world. The way that technology has changed combat makes people worry about the balance of power and how easy it is to use destructive force.

The digital gap is an important thing to think about when looking at how technology and power are connected. On a world level, power imbalances are caused by different levels of access to technology. People who don't have access are left behind and can't fully take part in the digital change. Lack of access has an impact on people's ability to learn, find work, and improve their social and economic situation. Since power is becoming more and more tied to technological progress, closing the digital gap is essential for making society more fair.

As we look to the future, we have to guess how new tools might change the balance of power. Blockchain, virtual reality, and quantum computing are just a few of the technologies that could have big effects on our lives. We don't fully understand how these technologies will affect power yet, but they could change the way businesses work, social contracts are written, and power relationships as we know them.

In conclusion, it's impossible to overstate how much technical progress has changed the way power works.

Technology has a huge impact on our lives, from digital monitoring to access to information, from social media to automation. In a world where power and technology are becoming more and more connected, it is important to understand what this connection means and how it might change in the future.

Chapter Eight

The Power of Collective Action

The idea of collective action is very important for changing the way power is currently distributed. It is the force that comes out when people work together for a shared goal, using their combined strength to make real change. Collective action is strong because it can change the status quo and shake up the power dynamics that keep oppressive and unfair systems in place. It is a force that shakes the very roots of power structures and makes it possible for society to be more fair and just.

Throughout history, there have been many examples of groups that used collective action to successfully challenge existing power structures. Movements like the labor movement, the feminist movement, and the civil rights movement have shown how powerful it is for people to work together to change social norms and the way power works. These groups used a variety of tactics, such as protests, strikes, and organizing at the local level, to get a lot of people to demand change. By speaking with one voice, they were able to make big changes in society, breaking down obstacles and oppressive systems that had been in place for a long time.

The power of numbers is one of the most important ideas behind group action. The huge number of people involved in a collective action movement can change the way power works and force those in charge to listen to what the people want. Protests, boycotts, and other forms of mass action make a force that is hard to ignore, which puts pressure on institutions and people who make decisions. The power of these groups comes from the fact that they are led by the will of the people as a whole, who believe in their ability to make things better.

It's impossible to overstate how important social media is for getting people to work together and question power systems these days. Sites like Twitter and Facebook have become very useful for planning and coordinating large-scale protests. They've given people a way to talk about their lives, bring attention to social and political problems, and bring people together around the world. People from underrepresented groups may be able to use social media to make their opinions heard and get more resources and attention. But it's important to be aware that social media has some problems too, like the ability to spread false information and the danger of depending too much on digital platforms for group action.

Collective action is the only way to bring people from different backgrounds and hobbies together, which can help communities that aren't connected. People may have different goals, hobbies, or experiences, but when they work together, they can challenge the power structures that are in place. Collective action can help break down barriers and build stronger bonds by recognizing the power that comes from differences. Collective action brings people together despite their differences to make a force that is stronger than the sum of its parts. This breaks down current power structures and makes way for a society where everyone feels welcome.

Collective actions could have an even bigger effect in the future, as new technologies, shifting social norms, and changing power structures change the movements environment. As technology keeps bringing people together and making their views heard, people working together will be able to do even more. We need to stay positive and inspired by the power of working together to change and challenge the power systems that are in place. We can keep making progress toward a more fair and just society by using the power of collective action.

Chapter Nine

Conclusion

Power is a complex force that comes from going through hard times and not giving up. It has shaped empires, changed lives, and changed history. The pursuit of power requires a deep understanding of its complexities and a commitment to using it responsibly.

50 Shades of Power is an attempt to have a thorough look at power, using psychology, history, sociology, and philosophy to reveal hidden mechanisms. It is not a book about tricks or short cuts to power, but a compass for people to navigate the complicated world of authority and influence. The book aims to create a world where power can be used with grace and

wisdom, fostering growth and illuminating the true potential of individuals.

Have you identified the power that resonates with you? I would be happy to hear what you got from this book. You can share your insights or feedback by writing directly to me at *authormanhardeep@gmail.com*

9 798877 743823